W9-DBR-182

Practical English Workbook

Second Edition

Floyd C. Watkins
Emory University

William B. Dillingham
Emory University

John T. Hiers
Valdosta State College

Houghton Mifflin Company   Boston

Dallas   Geneva, Ill.   Hopewell, N.J.   Palo Alto   London

INSTRUCTIONAL SERVICE CENTER

Stained glass window on cover executed by Susan Heller-Moore and photographed by James Scherer.

Acknowledgment is made to the following source of reprinted materials:

From John Rockwell, "Blues, and Other Noises, in the Night." Copyright © 1976 by *Saturday Review*. All rights reserved. Reprinted with permission.

Copyright © 1982, 1978 by Houghton Mifflin Company.

All rights reserved. No part of this work may be reproduced or transmitted in any form or by any means, electronic or mechanical, including photocopying and recording, or by any information storage or retrieval system, except as may be expressly permitted by the 1976 Copyright Act or in writing by the publisher. Requests for permission should be addressed in writing to Houghton Mifflin Company, One Beacon Street, Boston, Massachusetts 02108.

Printed in the U.S.A.

ISBN: 0-395-31736-3

Contents

Clauses

Kinds of Sentences

Part 2 Sentence Errors   51

Chapter 3 Common Sentence Errors   52

Sentence Fragments   Comma Splices   Fused Sentences

Chapter 4 Verb Forms   61

Verbs

Tense and Sequence of Tenses   Voice   Subjunctive Mood

Chapter 5 Agreement: Subject and Verb   77

Chapter 6 Pronouns: Agreement and Reference   82

Antecedents   Correct Case

Chapter 7   Adjective or Adverb?   94

Adjectives and Adverbs Compared   Forms of the Comparative and Superlative

Part 3   Sentence Structure   99

Chapter 8   Choppy Sentences and Excessive Coordination   100

Subordination   Completeness   Comparisons   Consistency

Chapter 9   Position of Modifiers, Parallelism, Sentence Variety   121

Modifiers   Dangling Modifiers   Misplaced Modifiers, Squinting Modifiers   Separation of Elements   Parallelism   Sentence Variety

Part 4   Punctuation   147

Chapter 10   The Comma   148

Uses of the Comma   Unnecessary Commas

Chapter 11   Semicolon, Colon, Dash, Parentheses, Brackets   175

The Semicolon   The Colon   The Dash   Parentheses   Brackets

Chapter 12   Quotation Marks and End Punctuation   184

Quotation Marks   End Punctuation

Part 5   Mechanics   191

Chapter 13   The Dictionary   192

Chapter 14   Italics   196

Titles   Foreign Words   For Occasional Emphasis

Chapter 15   Spelling   202

Guides for Spelling   Hyphenation and Syllabication

Chapter 16   Apostrophes, Capitals, and Numbers   218

Apostrophes   Capital Letters   Abbreviations   Numbers

Part 6   Diction and Style   229

Chapter 17   Standard English   230

Improprieties   Idioms   Triteness   Correctness   Wordiness
Repetition

Chapter 18   Connotation, Figurative Language, and Vocabulary   274

Connotation   Figurative Language   Flowery Language

Chapter 19   Paragraph Unity   287

Cross-References to the *Practical English Handbook*, Sixth Edition   296

Preface

The organization of the Second Edition of the *Practical English Workbook* closely follows that of the *Practical English Handbook,* Sixth Edition. For those students who require more practice with basic skills, this workbook is designed to reinforce the instruction of the handbook with parallel lessons, additional examples, and varied exercises. Beginning with parts of speech, the workbook also provides lessons on parts of sentences, sentence errors, punctuation, mechanics, diction and style, and paragraph unity. The logical sequence of these lessons makes the *Practical English Workbook* adaptable to other texts as well as to independent study and laboratory instruction for students at all levels.

In this edition the instruction has been greatly expanded. More extensive examples—and full explanations of why an example is correct or incorrect—have been added, and most of the exercises have been completely revised. Sections on the use of the dictionary are new, and the lessons on paragraph unity are contemporary and lively. This edition of the *Practical English Workbook* is fundamentally a new book.

We have attempted to make the style of the *Practical English Workbook* concise and readable and to avoid the extremes of lazy colloquialism and rigid formality. Without being condescending or simplistic, the *Practical English Workbook* stresses clarity and precision.

Like the *Practical English Handbook,* the *Practical English Workbook* follows a traditional approach to grammar, punctuation, and syntax. We believe that this method has proven itself over the years the best means to call attention to writing problems and to improve the writing skills of students. This mainstream approach to grammar, punctuation, and syntax has dictated the workbook's methodology. We have worked toward stating the most useful rules in the simplest form possible and have stressed typical problems in both examples and exercises. Throughout the text, emphasis is upon building writing skills and developing the student's understanding of the well-established practices governing the use of the English language.

We are deeply indebted to Professor James O. Williams of Valdosta State College for his aid and advice. We also wish to thank Nancy Beere, Temple University, for her thoughtful review of the manuscript.

F. C. W.   W. B. D.   J. T. H.

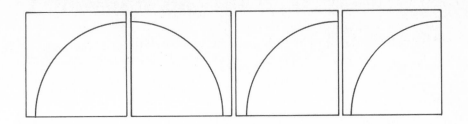

Grammar

The Parts of Speech   1

The English language has eight parts of speech: nouns, pronouns, verbs, adjectives, adverbs, conjunctions, prepositions, and interjections.

Nouns

Nouns are words that name. There are five kinds of nouns: proper nouns, common nouns, collective nouns, abstract nouns, and concrete nouns.

(a) **Proper nouns** name particular persons, places, or things (Thomas Edison, Chicago, Kleenex).

   Commodore Perry sailed to *Japan* on the *U.S.S. Mississippi.*

(b) **Common nouns** name one or more of a class or group *(doctor, pilots, artists).*

   The *students* walked to their *classroom.*

(c) **Collective nouns** name a whole group, though they are singular in form *(senate, jury, clergy).*

   The *herd* is grazing peacefully.

(d) **Abstract nouns** name concepts, beliefs, or qualities *(truth, energy, humor).*

   Loyalty is a noble *virtue.*

(e) **Concrete nouns** name things experienced through the senses *(fire, coffee, roses).*

   I prepared a small *plate* of *crackers* and *cheese.*

Pronouns

There are seven kinds of pronouns. Most pronouns are used in place of nouns, although indefinite pronouns do not refer to any particular noun.

(a) **Demonstrative pronouns** summarize in one word the content of a statement that has already been made. They may be singular *(this, that)* or plural *(these, those).*

   Many people crowded on the bus. *This* meant I would not find a seat.

(b) **Indefinite pronouns** do not indicate a particular person or thing. They are usually singular. The most common indefinite pronouns are *any, anybody, anyone, everybody, everyone, neither, none, one,* and *some.*

   Anyone can enter the contest by filling out an entry form.

(c) **Intensive pronouns** end in *-self* or *-selves (herself, themselves).* An intensive pronoun emphasizes a word that precedes it in the sentence.

2   Copyright © 1982 by Houghton Mifflin Company

She *herself* was surprised at her quick success.

The committee *itself* was confused.

(d) **Interrogative pronouns** *(what, which, who, whom, whose, whoever, whomever)* are used in questions.

Which is mine?

What are we going to do tonight?

(e) **Personal pronouns** usually refer to a person or group of people, but sometimes refer to an object or objects.

We need *her* on the team to help *us* play better.

Put *it* on the table.

	SINGULAR	PLURAL
First person	I, me, mine	we, us, ours
Second person	you, yours	you, yours
Third person	he, she, it, him, her, his, hers, its	they, them, theirs

(f) **Reflexive pronouns** end in *-self* or *-selves* and indicate that the action of the verb returns to the subject.

He caught *himself* making the same mistake twice.

The broken flywheel caused the machine to destroy *itself*.

(g) **Relative pronouns** *(who, whom, whoever, whomever, whichever, whose, that, what, which)* are used to introduce dependent adjective and noun clauses.

You can eat the pie *that is in the refrigerator.* (adjective clause modifying *pie,* introduced by the relative pronoun *that*)

I know *what will help you.* (noun clause used as object of verb *know*)

Verbs

Verbs express an action, a state of being, or a condition.

The bus *screeched* to a stop. (verb showing *action*)

The capital of Missouri *is* Jefferson City. (verb showing *state of being*)

Verbs that show *condition* are called **linking verbs.** The most common linking verbs are forms of the verb *to be (is, are, was, were).* Other linking verbs are *seem, become, look, appear, feel, sound, smell,* and *taste.*

The passengers *were* sleepy. (linking verb showing condition of sleep)

Main verbs may have **auxiliary verbs,** or helpers, such as *are, have, may, will.*

The school band *has* left the field.

Adjectives

Adjectives are descriptive words that modify nouns or pronouns. The **definite article** *the* and the **indefinite articles** *a* and *an* are also classified as adjectives.

The howling dog kept us awake.

Predicate adjectives follow linking verbs and modify the subject of the sentence.

This milk is *sour*.

The dog looks *old*.

Some **possessive adjectives** are similar to pronouns: *my, your, her, his, its, their*. These adjectives refer to specific nouns just as pronouns do but function as adjectives.

Your dinner is ready.

Demonstrative adjectives and demonstrative pronouns have the same forms: *this, that, these, those*. (See demonstrative pronouns, p. 2.)

This comment is helpful. (*This* modifies *comment*.)

This is a helpful comment. (*This* is used here as a demonstrative pronoun.)

Indefinite adjectives resemble indefinite pronouns: *some, many, most, every*.

Every employee received a bonus.

Adverbs

Adverbs describe, qualify, or limit verbs (and verbals), adjectives, and other adverbs.

She left *quickly*. (adverb—modifies a verb)

Talking *fast*, she soon was out of breath. (adverb—modifies the verbal *talking*)

The train was *very* late. (adverb—modifies the adjective *late*)

We'll be through *very* soon. (adverb—modifies another adverb *soon*)

Many adverbs are formed by adding *-ly* to adjectives; others express place or time: *soon, later, always, forever, there, out*.

Take the dog *out*.

Conjunctions

Conjunctions connect words, phrases, and clauses.

Coordinating conjunctions—*and, but, or, nor, for, yet*—connect sentence elements that are of equal rank.

John *and* Mary are visiting us today. (conjunction joining two nouns)

4
Copyright © 1982 by Houghton Mifflin Company

We needed to talk to you, *but* your telephone was always busy. (conjunction joining two independent clauses)

Subordinating conjunctions introduce a dependent element in a sentence—that is, one that cannot stand alone as a sentence. Some common subordinating conjunctions are *although, because, if, since, unless,* and *when.*

When we finished the test. (dependent element, not a sentence)

When we finished the test, we turned in our papers. (dependent element joined to independent clause to form a complete sentence)

We were tired *because we had studied all night.* (dependent element joined to independent clause to form a complete sentence)

Prepositions

Prepositions are connective words that join nouns or pronouns to other words in a sentence to form a unit (called a **prepositional phrase**). Prepositional phrases usually function as either adjectives or adverbs. Some prepositions are *above, at, before, by, from, in, into, of, over, through, up,* and *with.*

The jet flew *through the clouds.* (*Through the clouds* is a prepositional phrase used as an adverb to modify the verb *flew.*)

The woman *in the car* is my mother. (*In the car* is a prepositional phrase used as an adjective to modify the noun *woman.*)

Some words that resemble prepositions function as adverbs:

Go out. (*out* used as adverb)

Go out the door. (*out* used as preposition)

Interjections

Interjections are words that express surprise or strong emotions. They may stand alone or be part of a sentence.

Wow!

Well, you should have been more careful.

Copyright © 1982 by Houghton Mifflin Company

Parts of Speech: Nouns 1.1

▶ *Underline the words used as nouns in the following sentences.*

EXAMPLE

Despite its obvious dangers, skydiving continues to be a very popular recreation.

The sheep dog worked the flock with ease.

Thomas Jefferson was an architect, an inventor, and a politician.

1. Tourism is an important industry in many states.

2. The council is expected to approve the construction of lighted playgrounds and a landscaped industrial complex.

3. The "unsinkable" *Titanic* sank shortly after striking an iceberg.

4. The city of the future will have pedestrian parks, suspended monorail systems, and enclosed shopping centers, some of which will include fountains, sculptures, and bandstands.

5. Montana elected Jeannette Rankin to Congress, and she became the first woman to serve in the House of Representatives.

6. Once a community of old houses and bustling small businesses, this neighborhood is now marked by apartments, four-lane highways, and malls.

7. The mourning dove is rapidly becoming an urban bird, gradually following the ways of its cousin, the rock dove—commonly known as a pigeon.

8. When exploration of space became a reality, astronomy attracted many students.

9. Handball, golf, and tennis have become very popular as the modern family searches for recreational variety.

10. Solar energy and nuclear energy may supply electrical power in the twenty-first century; however, giant windmills also may dot the

coastal regions of New England and the Middle Atlantic States to provide additional energy.

Copyright © 1982 by Houghton Mifflin Company

Parts of Speech: Pronouns 1.2

▶ *Underline the pronouns in the following sentences.*

EXAMPLE

Those who visit the National Archives discover for themselves the living past.
(demonstrative, relative, reflexive pronouns)

She asked whoever was in charge to come forward. (personal, relative pronouns)

1. The judges themselves could not follow the complicated instructions given by the director of the tournament.

2. The Alps, the Rockies, the Urals—these are good mountain ranges
   for skiing and climbing.

3. Almost anyone can appreciate the United Way, for it provides funds
   for humanitarian causes.

4. Rand Corporation, which was established in 1948, researches and
   analyzes problems for governmental officials to help them make
   sound decisions.

5. "Who is willing to go on this dangerous expedition with them?"

6. Those who expect perfection often frustrate themselves.

7. Whoever said she was afraid of hard work did not know her very
   well.

8. If we sent a radio signal to the closest star system and there were
   someone to answer, the lapsed time before we received a message
   would be nine years.

9. A famous poem by Robert Frost begins, "Whose woods these are I
   think I know."

10. The trainer herself could not persuade the frightened horses to en-
    ter the arena, which they had never seen before.

Copyright © 1982 by Houghton Mifflin Company

Parts of Speech: Verbs   1.3

▶ *Underline the verbs in the following sentences.*

EXAMPLE

The astronauts <u>waited</u> several hours.

Mission Control <u>resumed</u> the countdown.
Most of the dogs at the show <u>were</u> retrievers.

1. With great speed the enormous tire rolled away.
2. The book club chose an excellent novel this month.
3. Of all the candidates for mayor, she was the most articulate.
4. The hail pelted the crops and shredded the leaves.
5. The group on the beach huddled close to the fire and enjoyed the winter night.
6. Recreational vehicles make camping a wonderful experience.
7. The famous American botanist Luther Burbank was called the "plant wizard."
8. At the beginning of this century immigrants to America needed twenty-five dollars as an indication of self-sufficiency.
9. Do most mutual funds require minimum investments?
10. Did the electrician follow your directions, or did he find the house by himself?

Copyright © 1982 by Houghton Mifflin Company

Parts of Speech: Adjectives 1.4

▶ *Underline the words used as adjectives in the following sentences. Remember that* articles (a, an, the) *are also classified as adjectives.*

EXAMPLE

A<u>n</u> <u>abstract</u> argument without <u>a</u> <u>concrete</u> illustration indicates <u>vague</u> thinking.

1. The puzzled historian stared at the faded painting of the royal couple.

2. At the circus the children laughed and clapped as fifteen clowns emerged from the small car.

3. In 1904 the famous Geronimo rode in the inaugural parade of Theodore Roosevelt.

4. Some winter campers use small propane heaters to combat cold weather.

5. While traveling through Alabama, we stopped at a popular museum in Tuskegee to see splendid exhibits depicting achievements of famous black Americans.

6. The hissing, sputtering fire told the group sitting beneath the thick cover of the elm trees that the rain had come.

7. Five tiny faces peered out of the rickety tree house as the rising wail of a siren preceded the huge red fire engine down the street.

8. Collectors of coins keep in touch with fellow enthusiasts through personal correspondence, small local clubs, and national magazines.

9. A complex, sophisticated, spectacular, and mysterious system of computers directed the first space shuttle into orbit.

10. The babies of cottontail rabbits are born blind and hairless.

Copyright © 1982 by Houghton Mifflin Company

Parts of Speech: Adverbs 1.5

▶ *Underline the words used as adverbs in the following sentences.*

EXAMPLE

Long-distance runners <u>often</u> are <u>exceptionally</u> versatile athletes who <u>simply</u> prefer the <u>less</u> publicized atmosphere of track and field.

1. The office staff hastily prepared a party when they heard their boss had been promoted.

2. The ambulance moved quickly into the street and narrowly missed an oncoming car.

3. Speaking very softly, the diner apologetically asked for more coffee.

4. Swiftly crossing the airport waiting room, the traveler barely missed a crowd of passengers preparing to board the flight.

5. Some modern artists paint boldly and often distort external reality to emphasize old truths in a stark, effective way.

6. Soon after the sky began to darken, vicious winds angrily beat against the small cabin.

7. While carefully examining the walls of the ancient building, the archaeologist suddenly discovered a small cache of coins that easily were over two thousand years old.

8. The flowers were covered partially by late spring frost that quickly melted when the sun rose.

9. As the morning fog quietly rolled in over the city, the traffic gradually slowed.

10. Speaking much too softly, the new mayor barely could be heard by the spirited crowd.

Copyright © 1982 by Houghton Mifflin Company

Parts of Speech: Conjunctions, Prepositions, and Interjections   1.6

▶ *Underline prepositions in the following sentences once, conjunctions twice, and interjections three times.*

EXAMPLE

Ah, the breezes of spring seem like the soft sighs of lovers or the breaths of children in pleasant sleep.

1. Although the passengers escaped injury in the accident, they both claimed that their lives flashed before their eyes while they were in danger.

2. During the summer the rain came nearly every day, and the fields were all like shallow lakes.

3. Alas, the present is fleeting into the past without a sound.

4. Beneath the great oak in the village, citizens had gathered for town meetings since the eighteenth century.

5. Well, only an uninformed person would make such a statement.

6. Many people in the audience did not hear much of the lecture because the technicians never arrived to connect the public-address system and the speaker's voice did not carry throughout the hall.

7. Oh, the less said the better sometimes, for neither words nor actions always express our deepest emotions.

8. Across the country, buyers hurried to stores to purchase the new vitamin capsules by the dozens of bottles.

9. In the middle of his speech, the lecturer realized that some of the pages of his text were missing.

10. In the afternoon when the storm had subsided, the shells were thickly scattered along one section of the beach, but beyond that area none could be found.

Copyright © 1982 by Houghton Mifflin Company

Same Word; Several Functions   1.7

▶ *Many words can function as several parts of speech. Compose very brief sentences with the following words, illustrating the parts of speech in parentheses. If necessary, check a dictionary.*

EXAMPLE

rake (noun) *The hero of the story evolves from a rake to a gentleman.*

rake (verb) *The children raked the field and made a baseball diamond.*

1. like (preposition) _____

_____

_____

(adjective) _____

_____

_____

(verb) _____

_____

_____

2. sample (noun) _____

_____

_____

(verb) _____

_____

_____

(adjective) _____

_____

_____

3. well (noun) _____

   _____

   _____

   (interjection) _____

   _____

   _____

   (adverb) _____

   _____

   _____

4. major (adjective) _____

   _____

   _____

   (noun) _____

   _____

   _____

   (verb) _____

   _____

   _____

5. open (adjective) _____

   _____

   _____

   (noun) _____

   _____

   _____

   (verb) _____

   _____

   _____

6. border (noun) _____

   _____

Copyright © 1982 by Houghton Mifflin Company

(verb) _____

_____

_____

(adjective) _____

_____

7. quiet (noun) _____

_____

_____

(adjective) _____

_____

_____

(adverb) _____

_____

_____

8. quick (noun) _____

_____

_____

(adjective) _____

_____

_____

(adverb) _____

_____

_____

9. paper (noun) _____

_____

_____

(verb) _____

_____

(adjective) _____

10. down (noun) _____

(verb) _____

(preposition) _____

Copyright © 1982 by Houghton Mifflin Company

Subjects and Predicates

A sentence has a complete meaning and can stand on its own. Its essential parts are its subject and predicate.

A **subject** does something, has something done to it, or is described.

The *woman* is reading. (subject acting)

Books are read. (subject acted upon)

Books are interesting. (subject described)

A **predicate** says something about the subject.

The woman *is reading.*

Books *are sources of information.*

Books *are interesting.*

The **simple subject** usually consists of one word. The **complete subject** consists of all the words that function together as the subject.

The *house* is dark. (simple subject)

The old house is dark. (complete subject)

When similar units of a sentence are linked together and function together, they are termed **compound.**

The automobile and *the truck* stopped. (compound subject)

The verb in a sentence is called the **simple predicate.** The simple predicate, its modifiers, and any complements are called the **complete predicate.**

Harry *finished* his work. (simple predicate)

Harry *finished his work.* (complete predicate)

Complements

Complements complete the meaning of the sentence. They are predicate adjectives, predicate nominatives, direct objects, and indirect objects. Predicate adjectives and predicate nominatives are also called **subjective complements.**

Predicate adjectives follow linking verbs and describe the subject.

Our neighbor is *tall.* (predicate adjective describing *neighbor*)

The fresh tomato tastes *sweet.* (predicate adjective after linking verb)

Predicate nominatives are nouns that follow linking verbs and rename the subject.

Our neighbor is an *actor*. (predicate nominative renaming neighbor)

Direct objects receive the action of a transitive verb.

We played *scrabble*. (direct object telling what was played)

Indirect objects receive the action of the verb indirectly. When the preposition *to* or *for* is understood, the word is an indirect object. A sentence with an indirect object must also have a direct object.

Sheila gave *me* a present. (indirect object telling *to whom* the present was given)

Copyright © 1982 by Houghton Mifflin Company

The Parts of Sentences   2.1

▶ *Underline the simple or compound subjects once and the simple or compound predicates twice. Identify complements with the abbreviations **p.a.** (predicate adjective), **p.n.** (predicate nominative), **d.o.** (direct object), and **i.o.** (indirect object) above the appropriate words.*

EXAMPLE
                             d.o.
Tourists <u>took</u> many photographs of the new office complexes.

1. Few receive great honors in their lifetimes.

2. William H. Seward purchased Alaska for the United States in 1867.

3. Technological advancements with microwaves have revolutionized long-distance communications.

4. At the end of the narrow footpath, the hikers discovered a broad meadow.

5. The famous physician told the young medical students many harrowing stories about the earliest methods of treating diseases.

6. The rodeo officials gave the competitors a list of rule changes before the first event.

7. Sales representatives often give buyers discounts on higher-priced appliances.

8. Clouds are minute particles of water or ice.

9. The color of the canyon walls became a brilliant orange from the setting sun.

10. The blackberry is edible, and it is used often in pastries.

Copyright © 1982 by Houghton Mifflin Company

The Parts of Sentences 2.2

▶ *Underline the simple or compound subjects once and the simple or compound predicates twice. Identify complements with the abbreviations* ***p.a.*** *(predicate adjective),* ***p.n.*** *(predicate nominative),* ***d.o.*** *(direct object), and* ***i.o.*** *(indirect object) above the appropriate words.*

EXAMPLE

$$p.a.$$

The <u>researchers</u> and <u>photographers</u> <u><u>were</u></u> hungry after the field trip.

1. The children in the band especially like the drums.

2. His gestures showed us his excitement.

3. Hikers along the Appalachian Trail often prepare extensively for their treks.

4. The restoration of antique cars has become a hobby of growing popularity, and it offers lucrative investment possibilities.

5. The Pueblo Indians of the American Southwest have preserved their cultural integrity, their links with the past.

6. *Voyager 2* provided the television networks with new photographs of the moons of Jupiter.

7. During the summer many agricultural jobs are available for high school students.

8. Johns Hopkins University, of Baltimore, Maryland, was patterned after the great German universities of the nineteenth century.

9. The children's grandfather brought each of them a sack of candy.

10. The League of Women Voters published the names of candidates and listed each one's position on the major issues.

Copyright © 1982 by Houghton Mifflin Company

Phrases

A phrase is a group of words that does not have both a subject and verb.

A **noun phrase** consists of a noun and its modifiers.

The new computer programmer started yesterday.

An **appositive phrase** renames a noun.

The Pentagon, *the largest office building in the world,* is located in Washington, D.C.

A **verb phrase** consists of the main verb and its helping verbs.

The house *is being painted.*

Prepositional phrases function as adjectives or adverbs.

The door *to the closet* is open. (adjectival phrase modifying *door*)

The rain fell *in the park.* (adverbial phrase modifying *fell*)

Verbals and Verbal Phrases

A verbal is formed from a verb. Three kinds of verbals are gerunds, participles, and infinitives.

Gerund

A gerund always ends in *-ing* and functions as a noun.

Swimming is fun. (gerund as subject)

Swimming in the high surf after the storm is exciting. (gerund phrase as subject)

Participle

Participles usually end in *-ing, -ed, -d, -t,* or *-n.* They function as adjectives.

Tired of reading, he decided to take a short walk. (modifies *he; tired of reading* is the complete participial phrase)

Troubled by her lack of progress, she decided to replan her time. (modifies *she; troubled by her lack of progress* is the complete participial phrase)

Infinitive

Infinitives begin with *to,* which is followed by a verb. They function as nouns, adjectives, or adverbs.

To show the new student around our school took time. (infinitive phrase as subject)

Camera cases *to be carried on the trip* must be waterproof. (infinitive phrase as adjective)

To be certain of lodging, one should make reservations. (infinitive phrase as adverb)

Copyright © 1982 by Houghton Mifflin Company

Phrases 2.3

▶ *On the blank lines, indicate whether the underlined phrase is used as subject, modifier, or verb, and indicate its function in the sentence.*

EXAMPLE

Using credit cards is a way *of life* for modern Americans.

modifier—prepositional phrase modifying noun way.

The scientists, *concerned about the potential hazards,* wanted the latest research findings made public.

modifier—participial phrase modifying noun scientists.

1. Most cities own delicate instruments <u>designed to monitor air pollution.</u>

⎯⎯⎯⎯⎯⎯⎯⎯⎯⎯⎯⎯⎯⎯⎯⎯⎯⎯⎯⎯⎯⎯⎯⎯⎯⎯⎯⎯⎯⎯⎯⎯⎯⎯⎯

2. The old trunk <u>in the attic</u> contained a precious collection of nineteenth-century books.

⎯⎯⎯⎯⎯⎯⎯⎯⎯⎯⎯⎯⎯⎯⎯⎯⎯⎯⎯⎯⎯⎯⎯⎯⎯⎯⎯⎯⎯⎯⎯⎯⎯⎯⎯

3. Patients under anesthetics <u>can be</u> aware of the conversation of the operating team.

⎯⎯⎯⎯⎯⎯⎯⎯⎯⎯⎯⎯⎯⎯⎯⎯⎯⎯⎯⎯⎯⎯⎯⎯⎯⎯⎯⎯⎯⎯⎯⎯⎯⎯⎯

4. Clearly understanding the surgeon's comments during the operation is absolutely essential <u>for the surgical team.</u>

⎯⎯⎯⎯⎯⎯⎯⎯⎯⎯⎯⎯⎯⎯⎯⎯⎯⎯⎯⎯⎯⎯⎯⎯⎯⎯⎯⎯⎯⎯⎯⎯⎯⎯⎯

5. <u>Many ancient civilizations</u> had remarkably accurate methods for measuring time.

⎯⎯⎯⎯⎯⎯⎯⎯⎯⎯⎯⎯⎯⎯⎯⎯⎯⎯⎯⎯⎯⎯⎯⎯⎯⎯⎯⎯⎯⎯⎯⎯⎯⎯⎯

6. The chinook winds whip down the eastern slopes of the Rocky Mountains and sweep <u>across the vast prairies.</u>

⎯⎯⎯⎯⎯⎯⎯⎯⎯⎯⎯⎯⎯⎯⎯⎯⎯⎯⎯⎯⎯⎯⎯⎯⎯⎯⎯⎯⎯⎯⎯⎯⎯⎯⎯

7. Construction <u>of the new civic center and parkway</u> revived the sagging economy of downtown businesses.

8. On each side of the highway were hundreds of billboards <u>advertising everything</u> from modern motels to roadside stands that sell fresh fruit and bedspreads.

9. Many auto mechanics <u>have returned</u> to school to study electronics; thus they will be able to repair the electronic parts being built into new automobiles.

10. <u>The tour bus</u> stopped in Savannah so that the tourists could visit the beautiful old homes and the sections of town that date back to the last part of the eighteenth century.

 Copyright © 1982 by Houghton Mifflin Company

Phrases 2.4

▶ *Write sentences containing the following words in the prescribed phrases.*

1. *concerned;* participial phrase modifying a subject and placed before the verb

   _____

   _____

   _____

2. *to hear;* infinitive phrase used as an object

   _____

   _____

   _____

3. *giving;* gerund phrase used as an object of a preposition

   _____

   _____

   _____

4. *through;* prepositional phrase

   _____

   _____

   _____

5. *from;* prepositional phrase

   _____

   _____

   _____

6. *have been restored;* verb phrase

   _____

   _____

   _____

7. *was complicating;* verb phrase

_____

_____

_____

8. *except;* prepositional phrase

_____

_____

_____

9. *officer;* noun phrase

_____

_____

_____

10. *performing;* gerund phrase as subject of sentence

_____

_____

_____

11. *was cautioned;* verb phrase

_____

_____

_____

12. *walking;* gerund phrase as subject of sentence

_____

_____

_____

13. *tall clown;* noun phrase

_____

_____

14. *assuming;* participial phrase

_____

_____

Copyright © 1982 by Houghton Mifflin Company

15. *during;* prepositional phrase

_____

_____

16. *to ask;* infinitive phrase as an object

_____

_____

17. *over;* prepositional phrase

_____

_____

18. *overcome;* verb phrase

_____

_____

19. *lecture;* noun phrase

_____

_____

20. *discover;* verb phrase

_____

_____

Copyright © 1982 by Houghton Mifflin Company

Verbals and Verbal Phrases   2.5

▶ *Underline verbals and verbal phrases in the following sentences. Name the verbal, its part of speech, and its function.*

EXAMPLE

<u>Finding</u> the <u>current</u> too <u>strong</u>, the swimmer shouted for help.

participle used as adjective to modify noun swimmer.

1. Millions of Americans enjoy working crossword puzzles.

   _____

2. Stargazing on late summer nights can be delightful.

   _____

3. Determined by color, cut, and size, the price of diamonds varies greatly.

   _____

4. Dating on a tight budget is a universal problem.

   _____

5. Racing steeds are valuable investments, affording their owners pleasure as well as profit.

   _____

6. To honor one's ancestors is part of Japanese tradition.

   _____

7. Among the millions of stars hurtling through space may lie other planets with conditions suitable for life.

   _____

8. In the next decade most people will need to build smaller houses.

   _____

9. Many students finance their college educations by finding on-campus jobs.

   _____

10. Abandoning his chopsticks, the guest asked the waiter for a knife and fork.

   _____

11. People came from several states to hear their favorite entertainers.

   _____

12. Old houses of Maine's coastal villages often have staircases carved by ship's carpenters.

   _____

13. Using ultrasonic techniques, doctors can detect possible birth defects.

   _____

14. One purpose of the National Endowment for the Humanities is to foster an awareness of our cultural inheritance.

   _____

15. Peruvian Indians may support their families by weaving colorful ponchos.

   _____

16. Shrimp fishermen do not support further draining of marshes.

   _____

17. A major goal of psychology is learning how emotions influence behavior.

   _____

18. Archeologists, working under strenuous conditions in the Arctic, discovered toy dolls over five hundred years old.

   _____

19. To enjoy television one needs a comfortable couch and a variety of snacks.

   _____

20. The employees to be selected for awards must excel in sales.

   _____

   Copyright © 1982 by Houghton Mifflin Company

Clauses

Clauses are groups of words with subjects and predicates. Clauses are either independent or dependent.

An **independent clause** can stand alone as a complete sentence. Two or more independent clauses may be linked (1) by coordinating conjunctions *(and, but, or, nor, for)* and a comma, (2) by a semicolon, or (3) by a semicolon and a **conjunctive adverb** (such as *however, therefore, moreover, nevertheless, otherwise*).

The circus is over, **and** the workers are cleaning the grounds. (two independent clauses connected by a comma and a coordinating conjunction)

The river was crowded with barges; each one of them was piled high with coal from the mines of Kentucky and West Virginia. (two independent clauses joined by a semicolon)

Low clouds obscured much of the mountain; **however,** the snow-covered peak sparkled in the bright sunlight. (two independent clauses joined by a semicolon and a conjunctive adverb)

A **dependent clause** may function as a noun, adjective, or adverb.

Who the guest speaker was to be is a mystery. (noun clause as subject)

Anyone *who helps* will be paid. (adjective clause modifying *anyone*)

When the game started, we stood up. (adverb clause modifying *stood*)

Copyright © 1982 by Houghton Mifflin Company

Clauses 2.6

▶ *Write whether the dependent clauses are used as nouns, adjectives, or adverbs. Remember that dependent clauses can be parts of independent clauses.*

EXAMPLE

Although the horse ran well, she placed third.   *adverb*

What the speaker said could not be heard. (dependent clause used as subject of independent clause)   *noun*

1. The comedian *who stepped to the microphone* seemed nervous and unsure of his material.   _____

2. The organization *that started the day-care center* took care of thirty children.   _____

3. *Since we moved to town,* five new families have moved into our neighborhood.   _____

4. *When the young reporter arrived,* she interviewed several celebrities.   _____

5. *Whoever decides to run for president* must file a financial statement with the Federal Election Commission.   _____

6. Parents *who store poisonous chemicals in locked cabinets* are protecting their children's lives.   _____

7. *When the use of ostrich feathers in fashions became popular a century ago,* many ranchers in the Southwest raised ostriches.   _____

8. *Why the poet failed to complete his epic* baffles many scholars.   _____

9. *Although the football team was inexperienced,* it won the state championship.   _____

10. *After the furniture store was renovated,* the owner held a gigantic sale.   _____

11. Preferred stocks are marketed to *whoever is willing to pay a premium for less risk.*   _____

12. Travelers' checks are honored at any bank *that sells them.*   _____

13. The crowd was refused admission to the rally *because the auditorium was filled.*   _____

14. *How the Federal Reserve will respond to inflationary pressures* is always of great interest to Wall Street.   _____

15. *That investments in health spas have dynamic potential for growth* is now obvious. _____
16. Most music lovers do not realize *that classical western music* is popular in the Far East. _____
17. Noncredit classes in making candles and caning chairs are well attended *because they are both practical and interesting.* _____
18. The peach growers could not decide *which variety they should plant.* _____
19. *If birdwatchers are to be successful,* they must be in the field quite early in the morning. _____

20. The chef wondered *if the soup had enough salt.* _____

 Copyright © 1982 by Houghton Mifflin Company

Clauses 2.7

▶ *Write sentences using the following coordinating or subordinating conjunctions or conjunctive adverbs to introduce dependent clauses or to connect independent clauses.*

EXAMPLES

if; to introduce a dependent clause

If the need arises, banks can borrow money from other banks to meet their financial obligations.

and; to connect two main clauses

The yellow fruit of the palm tree is tasty, and, according to some scientists, it is also nutritious.

1. *and;* to connect two main clauses

_____

_____

_____

2. *therefore;* to connect two main clauses

_____

_____

_____

3. *since;* to introduce a dependent clause

_____

_____

_____

4. *whoever;* to introduce a dependent clause

_____

_____

_____

5. *unless;* to introduce a dependent clause

_____

_____

6. *nevertheless;* to introduce an independent clause

_____

_____

7. *before;* to introduce a dependent clause

_____

_____

8. *because;* to introduce a dependent clause

_____

_____

9. *or;* to introduce an independent clause

_____

—_____

10. *otherwise;* to introduce an independent clause

_____

_____

_____

     Copyright © 1982 by Houghton Mifflin Company

Kinds of sentences

There are four kinds of sentences: simple, compound, complex, and compound-complex.

A **simple sentence** has one independent clause.

The President flew to Camp David. (one subject, one predicate)

The President and his advisers flew to Camp David and began work on the budget. (compound subject, compound predicate)

A **compound sentence** contains two or more independent clauses joined by coordinating conjunctions or semicolons.

The new art show at the museum opened today, and the crowd was immense. (two independent clauses joined by *and*)

The new art show at the museum opened today; the crowd was immense. (two independent clauses joined by a semicolon)

A **complex sentence** consists of one independent clause and one or more dependent clauses.

When the new art show at the museum opened, the crowd was immense. (dependent clause and independent clause)

A **compound-complex sentence** is a compound sentence with one or more dependent clauses.

When the play ended, the curtain closed, and the audience applauded loudly. (dependent clause, independent clause, independent clause)

Copyright © 1982 by Houghton Mifflin Company

Kinds of Sentences   2.8

▶ *Identify each of the following sentences as simple (s), compound (cd), complex (cx), or compound-complex (cd/cx).*

EXAMPLE

___S___ Bombay is the commercial center of India.

_____ 1. Saturn has no night because its rings continuously reflect the sun's light onto the surface of the planet.

_____ 2. The lights in the neighborhood went out when lightning hit the power line, but service was restored in less than an hour.

_____ 3. Near Gillette, Wyoming, we watched a large herd of American bison.

_____ 4. The fastest woman in the world, Wilma Rudolph, won three gold medals in the 1960 Olympics.

_____ 5. When scientists have a problem to solve, they often work on the theory that the simplest solution is the best.

_____ 6. The art auctioneer stepped to the podium, and then he asked his assistant to describe the first painting to be sold.

_____ 7. Fish swim in underground streams beneath the Sahara Desert.

_____ 8. The library was especially quiet, and many of the readers appeared to be dozing.

_____ 9. The water in the salt marshes along the southern Atlantic coast is replenished by the rising ocean tide.

_____10. The service in the restaurant was slow, and our dinners were cold when they arrived.

Copyright © 1982 by Houghton Mifflin Company

Kinds of Sentences   2.9

▶ *Identify each of the following sentences as simple (s), compound (cd), complex (cx), or compound-complex (cd/cx).*

EXAMPLE

_CX___ When the alarm rang, everybody rushed out.

_____ 1. The tarantula's greatest enemy is the digger wasp.

_____ 2. After the Independence Day picnic ended, we watched the fireworks.

_____ 3. European workers enjoy four or five weeks of paid annual vacation, but American workers average a mere ten days of paid vacation.

_____ 4. When we left for the beach, the sky was clear, but clouds began to gather early in the afternoon.

_____ 5. The novels of Mark Twain are well known in China.

_____ 6. There are dozens of variations of the game of chess.

_____ 7. John Muir was not the first to discover the Yosemite Valley, but his essays introduced the area to people throughout the country.

_____ 8. The late afternoon traffic barely moved; each car seemed to be attached to the cars before it and after it like a single segment in a large and unlikely earthworm.

_____ 9. After examining the face of the cliff for almost an hour, the climbers finally decided upon the best place to make their ascent.

_____10. Before the building could be occupied, the inspectors carefully examined each floor, and the fire department checked the sprinkler system.

Copyright © 1982 by Houghton Mifflin Company

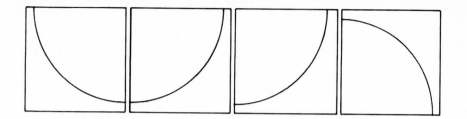

Sentence Errors

Sentence fragments

Sentence fragments are incomplete sentences and usually consist of dependent clauses, phrases, or any other word group that does not make a complete thought. Fragments should be corrected by making the sentence complete.

NOT

The car being old. (sentence fragment: We bought a new one. (complete sen-
noun and phrase)   tence)

BUT

The car being old, we bought a new one.

Comma splices

A comma splice occurs when two independent clauses are joined by a comma but have no coordinating conjunction *(and, or, nor, but)*.

NOT

The movie was very exciting, we discussed it as we drove home.

BUT

The movie was very exciting, **and** we discussed it as we drove home.

OR

The movie was very exciting; we discussed it as we drove home.

Fused sentences

A fused sentence occurs when two independent clauses have neither punctuation nor a conjunction between them.

NOT

He did not heed the warning he was not very careful.

BUT

He did not heed the warning, and he was not very careful.

Fused sentences also may be corrected by writing two sentences, by using either a semicolon or a comma and a conjunction, or by making one of the sentences into a dependent clause.

He did not heed the warning. He was not very careful. (two sentences)

He did not heed the warning; he was not very careful. (semicolon)

Because he was not careful, he did not heed the warning. (dependent clause)

    Copyright © 1982 by Houghton Mifflin Company

Sentence Fragments   3.1

▶ *In the blanks at the right identify the following as complete sentences or frag-*
ments.

EXAMPLE

Tune-ups save gas.   *sentence*

Because engines run more efficiently.   *fragment*

1. The last maple leaf fell to the ground.   _____

   Last Friday afternoon.   _____

2. A hamburger with mustard, lettuce, onion, and
   tomato.   _____

   He ate a quick lunch.   _____

3. Writing a letter home each week.   _____

   Keeping in touch with his family.   _____

4. The snow began to fall at dawn.   _____

   The schools closed at noon.   _____

5. Frightened by the thunder and lightning.   _____

   The puppy began to whimper.   _____

6. Left to amuse themselves while their parents
   talked.   _____

   After the children finished eating dinner.   _____

7. Because the prize was so large.   _____

   Contestants by the hundreds filling out forms. _____

8. Closing her office early on Friday.   _____

   Left for her vacation before dark.   _____

9. Few people listening to the concert.   _____

   The orchestra omitted an entire section of the
   last part of the symphony.   _____

10. The food in the restaurant being delicious.   _____

    She gladly paid the bill.   _____

   Copyright © 1982 by Houghton Mifflin Company

Sentence Fragments   3.2

▶ *Correct the following sentence fragments by joining them to the complete sentences.*

EXAMPLE

Some people think that to grow houseplants successfully, ~~C~~onvers~~ing~~ with them
and, in general, treat~~ing~~ them with affection.

(handwritten: one must / e)

1. Dust storms of North Africa and India are called by an Arabic name,
   haboobs. Meaning "to glow."

2. Pumpkin pie became a New England delicacy. After it was served
   at the second Thanksgiving feast in 1623.

3. Because he was caught without his wallet in his suit. The speeder
   pleaded with the police officer.

4. The descriptions of foods on American menus are usually more interesting than the foods themselves. Whereas on French menus the
   opposite is true.

5. To resolve bothersome details in the contract. The two lawyers
   worked late into the night.

6. Stretching the entire length of the continent. The Andes Mountains
   dominate the geography of western South America.

7. Once limited to the Western states. Rodeos now enjoy national popularity.

8. A few sea gulls wading on the beach. A solitary man gazing out
   across the horizon.

9. Although the *Star Wars* films have been immensely popular. They
   have yet to attract the number of fans that still enjoy the *Star Trek*
   television series.

10. Country-western music is now more popular than any other musi-
    cal style. Even more popular than the rock music that began in the
    1950s.

Copyright © 1982 by Houghton Mifflin Company

Comma Splices; Fused Sentences   3.3

Comma splices and fused sentences may be corrected in four principal ways:

1. Use a period and write two separate sentences.
2. Use a semicolon between two independent clauses.
3. Use a comma and a coordinating conjunction between two independent clauses.
4. Make one of the clauses dependent.

▶ *Indicate first whether each of the following is a comma splice or a fused sentence. Then in correcting the sentence, indicate the method you used by writing one of the four above numbers in the blank.*

EXAMPLE

Kansas City calls itself the City of Fountains, its goal is to build a new public fountain every year.　　　*Comma splice/2.*

1. The old movie theater downtown has been bought the new owners plan to convert the building into a small dinner theater.　　　_____

2. Many people think popcorn is a typical American food actually it was also popular in ancient times.　　　_____

3. The DC3 was first put into airline service in 1935 and many of these planes are still flying passengers.　　　_____

4. Constant reading will improve your vocabulary it will also improve your writing.　　　_____

5. Palindromes are a group of words that read the same forward and backward and they are very difficult to write.　　　_____

6. A great book delights us a lifetime a good book provides a moment's pleasure.　　　_____

7. Getting the right to vote is one thing, using it is another. _____

8. Many old cars use premium gasoline, which is now difficult to find they can be tuned to use regular or lower octane unleaded gasoline. _____

9. Scientists disagree on the source of intelligence, some say heredity is the main source, but others believe that the environment is more influential. _____

10. Norfolk, Phoenix, Philadelphia, Urbana, and Jacksonville are names of cities in five different states you can find towns bearing these names in New York state. _____

Copyright © 1982 by Houghton Mifflin Company

Comma Splices; Fused Sentences   3.4

▶ *Indicate whether each of the following is a comma splice or a fused sentence. In correcting the sentence, indicate the method you used by writing one of these four numbers in the blank: (1) corrected with a period (two sentences); (2) corrected with a semicolon; (3) corrected with a comma and a coordinating conjunction; (4) corrected by making one of the clauses dependent.*

1. Mosquitoes are found in various climates they thrive in Alaska as well as in the tropics. _____

2. Coast Guard cadets continue to train on sailing ships, thus they gain firsthand knowledge of traditional nautical lore. _____

3. A New York law at the turn of the century regulated automobiles under an ordinance applied to cattle it required a person to walk in front of the automobile carrying a red flag or lantern. _____

4. The Federal Reserve System controls the money supply for the entire United States local banks often borrow money from regional Reserve banks to ensure economic stability. _____

5. Between the winter and spring terms, thousands of college students go to Florida they especially like the beaches at Ft. Lauderdale, Clearwater, and Panama City. _____

6. One of the first commemorative stamps of 1981 honored Whitney Moore Young he founded the National Urban League. _____

7. The care of soft contact lenses usually requires about ten minutes a day over thirty years this will add up to two and a half months. _____

8. The *Flying Dutchman* is a legendary spectral ship, its captain, says the legend, must sail against the wind until Judgment Day.   _____

9. We knew the advertisement in the paper was incorrect it said the company wanted a "termite salesman" and a "customer service exterminator."   _____

10. Microsurgery now provides hope for accident victims after surgery many of them have regained complete mobility.   _____

Copyright © 1982 by Houghton Mifflin Company

Verbs
All verbs have three **principal parts:**

the **infinitive** *(concern)*

the **past tense** *(concerned)*

the **past participle** *(concerned)*.

These three forms are listed in the dictionary entry of each verb.

Regular, irregular verbs
Verbs may be regular or irregular in form. **Regular verbs** *(add, help, smile)* form the past tense and the past participle by adding *-d, -ed,* or sometimes *-t (kept, dreamt)*. The principal parts of *add* and *help* are *add, added, added; help, helped, helped.*

   Irregular verbs change form in the past tense and the past participle. Some irregular verbs *(begin, sing)* form the past tense and past participle by changing a single vowel *(sing, sang, sung)*. Other irregular verbs change more than one letter *(drive, drove, driven)*.

Transitive, intransitive verbs
Verbs also may be **transitive** (take an object) or **intransitive** (do not take an object).

TRANSITIVE VERB
The cook *tasted* the special *sauce*. *(Sauce* is the direct object.)

INTRANSITIVE VERB
The *rain fell* on the roof. *(Fell* does not take an object.)

   Especially troublesome are the irregular verbs *lie, lay; sit, set; rise, raise*. The verbs *lay, set,* and *raise* are transitive and take an object. The verbs *lie, sit,* and *rise* are intransitive and do not take an object.

   Each of these verbs has a specific meaning. *Lie* means to recline or to be situated; *lay,* to place. *Sit* means to be seated; *set,* to place or arrange. *Rise* means to get up; *raise* means to lift. When trying to decide upon the correct form of the verb, think of the meaning you want, whether the verb takes an object or not, the tense you need, and the correct principal part. (See also pp. 71–72.)

Lay the book on the table now. (present tense of *lay*)

She *laid* the book on the table and left. (past tense of *lay*)

The boat *lies* in the harbor. (present tense of *lie*)

The boat *lay* in the harbor for most of last week. (past tense of *lie*)

The waiter *set* the plate on the table. (*Plate* is the direct object.)

The archeologist *laid* the relics taken from the temple on the examining table. (*Relics* is the direct object.)

The honor guard will *raise* the flag. (*Flag* is the direct object.)

Some of the swimmers were *lying* on the beach. (*Lying* is intransitive and takes no object.)

The sewing basket was *sitting* in the corner. (*Sitting* is intransitive and takes no object.)

The speaker *rises* to address the meeting. (*Rises* is intransitive and takes no object.)

The principal parts of these verbs are included in the following list of difficult verbs.

Principal parts of some troublesome verbs

INFINITIVE	PAST TENSE	PAST PARTICIPLE
arise	arose	arisen
awake	awoke, awaked	awoke, awaked
be	was	been
bear (to carry)	bore	borne
bear (to give birth)	bore	born, borne
begin	began	begun
bid (offer)	bid	bid
bid (order or say)	bade	bidden
bite	bit	bitten, bit
blow	blew	blown
break	broke	broken
bring	brought	brought
burst	burst	burst
catch	caught	caught
choose	chose	chosen
come	came	come
deal	dealt	dealt
dig	dug	dug
dive	dived, dove	dived
do	did	done
drag	dragged	dragged
draw	drew	drawn
dream	dreamed, dreamt	dreamed, dreamt
drink	drank	drunk
drive	drove	driven
drown	drowned	drowned
eat	ate	eaten
fall	fell	fallen

Copyright © 1982 by Houghton Mifflin Company

INFINITIVE	PAST TENSE	PAST PARTICIPLE
find	found	found
flee	fled	fled
fly	flew	flown
forget	forgot	forgotten, forgot
freeze	froze	frozen
get	got	got, gotten
give	gave	given
go	went	gone
grow	grew	grown
hang (to execute)	hanged	hanged
hang (to suspend)	hung	hung
have	had	had
hear	heard	heard
know	knew	known
lay	laid	laid
lead	led	led
lend	lent	lent
let	let	let
lie	lay	lain
light	lighted, lit	lighted, lit
lose	lost	lost
pay	paid	paid
pay (ropes)	payed	payed
plead	pleaded, pled	pleaded, pled
prove	proved	proven, proved
raise	raised	raised
ride	rode	ridden
ring	rang, rung	rung
rise	rose	risen
run	ran	run
say	said	said
see	saw	seen
shine (to give light)	shone	shone
shine (to polish)	shined	shined
show	showed	shown, showed
shrink	shrank, shrunk	shrunk
sing	sang, sung	sung
sink	sank, sunk	sunk
sit	sat	sat
slide	slid	slid
sow	sowed	sown, sowed
speak	spoke	spoken
spit	spat, spit	spit, spat
spring	sprang, sprung	sprung
stand	stood	stood
steal	stole	stolen
stink	stank, stunk	stunk
swim	swam, swum	swum

INFINITIVE	PAST TENSE	PAST PARTICIPLE
swing	swung	swung
take	took	taken
tear	tore	torn

Copyright © 1982 by Houghton Mifflin Company

Verb Forms   4.1

▶ *Circle the correct verb form. Remember that intransitive verbs do* not *take direct objects. Remember that transitive verbs do take direct objects. Look for both the meaning and tense of the verb.*

EXAMPLE
The drum major (laid, lied) her baton on the ground. (The verb *laid* [past of *lay*] is transitive and takes the direct object *baton.*)

1. The judge (laid, lay) the old list of prospective jurors aside yesterday.

2. The editor (set, sat) a deadline for all features in the weekend edition.

3. Cranes can (raise, rise) heavy steel girders with relative ease.

4. All runners were told to (lie, lay) on their backs in the shade.

5. In the summer the sun (rises, raises) earlier than in the winter.

6. Bobcats often (sit, set) in high places to observe their territories in safety.

7. Until the storm subsided and the sea became calm, all passengers had (laid, lain) in their berths.

8. The hitter chose to (lay, lie) the bat on his shoulder and hope for a walk.

9. Animals often (sit, set) in mud to cool their dry skin and to protect themselves from insects.

10. Ships at sea (raise, rise) flags for communication.

Copyright © 1982 by Houghton Mifflin Company

Verb Forms 4.2

▶ *Circle the correct verb form.*

EXAMPLE

Retrieving the morning newspaper, the excited dog unintentionally (tore) torn) several pages.

1. Hitchhiking on interstate highways is (prohibit, prohibited) by federal law.

2. The people ran in terror when they (seen, saw) the flying saucers.

3. The worker's dirty clothes were (hung, hanged) on the back of the door.

4. The instructors (chose, choosed) sides and began the spelling competition.

5. After dinner she (go, went) to her room to do homework.

6. The candidate (begun, began) the campaign for Congress with an old-fashioned fish fry.

7. The burglar tried to deny that he had (stole, stolen) any jewelry.

8. At the park the children (slided, slid) down poles and climbed the monkey bars.

9. Yesterday he (laid, lay, lain) on his bed for three hours before he arose to eat.

10. To prevent pipes from (busting, bursting) on wintry nights, one should turn on outside spigots.

Copyright © 1982 by Houghton Mifflin Company

Verb Forms   4.3

▶ *Circle the correct verb form.*

EXAMPLE

The lifeguard (drug, (dragged)) the tired swimmer out of the water.

1. The rocks (falled, fell) from the cliff that (rised, rose) high above the valley.

2. Hurricane Camille, the most violent storm in recent history, (struck, striked) Gulfport, Mississippi, in 1969.

3. The campers (bade, baded) the cabin leaders goodbye and boarded their buses.

4. The competing relay teams (swam, swimmed) the race in record time.

5. The cowboys on the cattle drive had (rode, ridden) over four hundred miles.

6. Donkeys have been known to (bore, bear) twice their weight on their exceptionally strong backs.

7. The school board (came, come) to no decision on the issue of attendance regulations.

8. A newly discovered Roman vessel (sanked, sank) off the coast of Sicily sometime during the third century.

9. (Rang, Rung) only twice, the Liberty Bell now sits in Independence Hall in Philadelphia.

10. The trustees of the estate (paid, payed) all bills before disbursing legacies to the surviving relations.

Copyright © 1982 by Houghton Mifflin Company

Tense and sequence of tenses

Use verbs carefully to express distinctions of time. Avoid needless shifts of tense.

Usually the **present tense** expresses present time.

I *am going* home for lunch.

It also may show repeated action.

I *go* home for lunch.

Past tense shows past time.

I *went* home for lunch.

I *lay* in the sun for an hour. (past tense of verb *lie*)

Future tense shows future time.

I *shall go* home for lunch.

Perfect tenses

The three perfect tenses are used in well-defined sequences. They indicate time or action completed before another time or action.

1. Use **present perfect** with present.

   I *have asked* her to help, and she *refuses*.

2. Use **past perfect** with past.

   He *had wanted* to diet, but he *could* not.

3. Use **future perfect** with future.

   He *will have finished* before we *will begin*.

Infinitive

An infinitive usually takes the present tense when it expresses action that occurs at the same time as that of the controlling verb.

I *desired* to leave.

To complete the project, we *had* to work overtime yesterday.

Relationships between verbs should be logical and consistent.

NOT

I *walk* to the park and *had* lunch. (mixes present tense and past tense)

BUT

I *walked* to the park and *had* lunch. (past tense with past tense)

Voice

When the subject acts, the verb is in the **active voice.** When the subject is acted upon, the verb is in the **passive voice.** Use active voice except on those occasions when passive voice is required.

ACTIVE VOICE

Bill *gave* the book to Mary. (*Bill* acts.)

PASSIVE VOICE

The *book* was given to Mary. (*Book* is acted upon.)

Subjunctive mood

Use **subjunctive mood** to show wishes, commands, or conditions contrary to fact.

I wish I *were* rich. (wish)

The rules require that we *be* silent. (command)

If I *were* vacationing this week, I would be a happy person. (condition contrary to fact)

Copyright © 1982 by Houghton Mifflin Company

Tense and Sequence of Tenses   4.4

▶ *Correct the tense of the italicized verbs.*

EXAMPLE
                                     come
Azaleas are hearty plants which *have come* in several varieties.

1. Many weeks *pass* before the plans for the family's new home were finished.

2. In the middle of the afternoon, the girl climbed on her bicycle and *rides* to a nearby park.

3. The monthly bills were paid by the tenth of the month, whereas others *are paid* later.

4. She stood up to her employer without being afraid her criticism *reduces* her chances for promotion.

5. William Wordsworth, who *had lived* in the nineteenth century, became Poet Laureate of England.

6. Most visitors to the National Museum of Art prefer *to have had* more time for their visit.

7. Although the voting age *had been lowered* to eighteen, political scientists do not find that voters aged eighteen to twenty-one have had any effect on major election results.

8. Elephant herds haul away tons of silt from shallow water holes after their ritualistic herd baths; thus they *cleaned* the water and *created* water holes for other animals.

9. Fossil remains found in Antarctica *link* that continent with South America and have provided further evidence that the two land masses were once connected.

10. The term "tailgate trombone" once referred to a New Orleans trombonist who *plays* while standing on the back of a horse-drawn parade cart.

Copyright © 1982 by Houghton Mifflin Company

Voice   4.5

▶ *In the following sentences change the passive voice to active.*

EXAMPLE

Pride is instilled and friendships are promoted by voluntary neighborhood clean-up campaigns.

Voluntary neighborhood clean-up campaigns instill pride and promote friendships.

1. The swift stream was obstructed by salmon seeking their spawning grounds.

   _____

   _____

   _____

2. Backfires are often set by firefighters to combat large forest fires.

   _____

   _____

   _____

3. During millions of years natural sculptures have been carved by the wind in the majestic Grand Canyon.

   _____

   _____

   _____

4. The American traditions of philanthropy are continued today by large foundations as well as by generous individuals.

   _____

   _____

   _____

5. The seat chosen by the passenger was next to the window.

_____

_____

_____

6. Both hoecake and hardtack were invented by chuck-wagon cooks on cattle drives, who rarely had time to construct ovens.

_____

_____

_____

7. Flying squirrels are sighted commonly by visitors in the vast interior of the famous Okefenokee Swamp.

_____

_____

_____

8. Flight 481 was cleared for take-off by the air controller despite the heavy fog.

_____

_____

_____

9. The roots of some American music have been traced by musicologists back to British, Scottish, Welsh, and Irish folk songs.

_____

_____

_____

10. Fashions created by American designers are now bought by thousands of Europeans.

_____

_____

_____

Copyright © 1982 by Houghton Mifflin Company

Use singular verbs with singular subjects, and also use plural verbs with plural subjects. The *-s* or *-es* ending of the present tense of a verb in the third person *(he hopes, she stops)* indicates the singular. These endings for most nouns indicate the plural.

After compound subject
A **compound subject** with *and* usually takes a plural verb.

The city *and* the county *are* working together.

Collective nouns
Collective nouns (words like *family, flock, jury*) take a singular verb when referring to a group as a unit; they take a plural verb when the members of a group are treated individually.

My *family is* going on a trip this weekend.

My *family are* going to Hawaii, New Jersey, and Ohio on Labor Day.

After relative pronoun
After a relative pronoun (such as *who, which,* and *that*), the verb in the relative clause has the same person and number as the *antecedent* of the pronoun.

The sales *associate* who *is* here today represents a well-known firm.

After titles
A title of a book or a film is singular and requires a singular verb, even if it contains plural words and ideas.

Elements of Films is a useful book.

After *there, here*
In sentences that begin with **there** and **here,** the verb agrees with the subject of the sentence.

There *is* an old *mill* on this road.

There *are* many *challenges* in this project.

Word groups
Word groups, such as *in addition to* and *as well as,* do not change the number of the subject when they separate the subject and the verb.

State *officials* **as well as** our mayor *are examining* the problem.

The subject
The *subject* of the sentence, not the predicate noun, determines the number of the verb.

Her main *strength is* her ability to listen and to follow instructions.

When the subject in a sentence is *inverted*, the verb should agree with the *subject* of the sentence, not with the word that comes directly before the verb.

At the party *were Beatrice* and her *sister*. (Plural verb agrees with compound subject.)

Copyright © 1982 by Houghton Mifflin Company

Subject and Verb Agreement 5.1

▶ *Underline each subject once; then write the correct verb in the blank at the right.*

EXAMPLE

Periodic <u>tune-ups</u> and oil <u>changes</u> (helps, help) to ensure better gas mileage.

help

1. Almost everybody who attends college (want, wants) to avoid some course that seems too difficult.

   _____

2. Flying over the Rocky Mountains at dusk (is, are) a thrilling experience.

   _____

3. The family (is, are) going to Texas for a vacation.

   _____

4. The trial was so long that neither the judge nor the jury members (recall, recalls) all the evidence.

   _____

5. Here (is, are) the instructions for the examination.

   _____

6. A large crowd of people (was, were) at the sports arena.

   _____

7. We like everyone who (live, lives) in our neighborhood.

   _____

8. The convocation speaker as well as his wife and children (was, were) welcomed heartily by the audience.

   _____

9. What we really needed (was, were) more playgrounds and day-care centers.

   _____

10. There (is, are) many Americans who never bother to vote.

   _____

Copyright © 1982 by Houghton Mifflin Company

Subject and Verb Agreement 5.2

▶ *Underline each subject once; then write the correct verb in the blank at the right.*

EXAMPLE

All <u>members</u> of the council (is, are) present.   *are*

1. Both the employees and their boss (enjoy, enjoys) the annual Christmas party.   _____

2. Because of the storm neither the sailboat nor the small fishing boat (has, have) been able to leave port.   _____

3. Every one of the infants (learn, learns) how to swim under close supervision.   _____

4. The reader who wants to learn (choose, chooses) books carefully.   _____

5. The yo-yo, unlike the kite and the Frisbee, (is, are) a very ancient toy.   _____

6. The Science Club, which is sponsored by the Physics Department, (participate, participates) in the state Science Fair this weekend.   _____

7. On the list of bowlers in the tournament (was, were) Mary Ashley, Sonja Taylor, and Ruthie Johns, clearly the best in the region.   _____

8. The mural, viewed at the shopping center by the opening day crowd, (was, were) shocking to many.   _____

9. The desire to economize and help solve the energy shortage (sell, sells) many subcompact automobiles.   _____

10. Students' lack of desire to learn (cause, causes) teachers many heartaches.   _____

Pronouns: Agreement and Reference   6

Antecedents

Use singular pronouns to refer to singular antecedents, and use plural pronouns to refer to plural antecedents. Use a plural pronoun to refer to compound antecedents, except in those cases where the antecedents refer to the same person.

The *instructor* finished grading *her* papers.

The *instructors* finished grading *their* papers.

Which and *that* refer to animals and things. *Who* refers to people and sometimes to animals and things called by name. *That* refers to animals and things, but only sometimes to people.

The refrigerator *that (which)* I bought never needs defrosting.

The representative *who* sold it to me guaranteed the unit for ten years.

Pronouns should not refer vaguely to an entire sentence or to unidentified people. Do not make vague references using pronouns *they, them, it, you,* or *this.*

I have trouble taking standardized tests. *This* is my problem. (*This* is too vague.)

You know that *they* will do *it* every time. (*You, they,* and *it* are vague references.)

Make a pronoun refer clearly to one antecedent only.

UNCERTAIN

The man went to the doctor after *he* finished work. (Does *he* refer to *doctor* or *man*?)

CLEAR

After *he* finished work, the man went to the doctor. (*He* now clearly refers to *man.*)

Correct case

Pronouns have three cases: subjective, possessive, and objective. Personal pronouns and the relative pronoun *who* are inflected for these cases.

Subjective (acting)—I, he, she, we, they, who

Possessive (possessing)—my (mine), your (yours), his, her, (hers), its, our (ours), their (theirs), whose

Objective (acted upon)—me, him, her, us, them, one, whom

To determine case, find out how a word is used in its own clause—for example, whether it is a subject, a subjective complement, a possessive, or an object.

Use the **subjective case** for subjects and subjective complements.

 Copyright © 1982 by Houghton Mifflin Company

The contractor and *I* are about to reach an agreement. (Use *I*, not *me*, for the subject.)

The winner was *I*. (Use *I*, not *me*, after a linking verb.)

Use the **possessive case** to show ownership and for gerunds.

Their work was complete. (ownership)

Her rising to the presidency reflected hard work. (gerund)

The possessive forms of personal pronouns do *not* have apostrophes.

His is the best solution.

The possessive forms of indefinite pronouns *(everybody's, one's, anyone's)* do have apostrophes. Contractions such as *it's* (for *it is*) and *she's* (for *she is*) do have apostrophes.

Also use the **objective case** for the object of a preposition and for the subject of an infinitive.

Who among *us* will volunteer? (*Us* is the object of *among*.)

The college selected *her* to be the coach. (*Her* is the subject of the infinitive *to be*.)

For interrogative pronouns

The case of interrogatives *(who, whose, whom, what, which* used in questions) depends on their use in a specific clause.

Whom did the Senate confirm for the post? (Use *whom*, not *who*, because the interrogative pronoun is a direct object of *did confirm*.)

For appositives

For pronouns used as **appositives** (words that rename nouns or pronouns) use the same case as the noun or pronoun renamed.

Only we—Sharon and *I*—were excused. (*Sharon* and *I* rename the subject *we;* hence, use *I*, not *me*.)

The instructor excused two of us, Sharon and *me*. (*Sharon* and *me* rename the object of the preposition *of;* hence, use the objective case.)

After *than, as*

The correct case of a pronoun used after *than* or *as* is determined by completing the missing verb of the clause:

Margaret is taller than I. (*Than I am* is the complete clause; *I* is the subject of clause.)

She worked harder than you or I. (*than you or I worked*)

This crisis hurt him more than her. (*more than it hurt her; her* is the object)

Copyright © 1982 by Houghton Mifflin Company

Pronouns: Agreement and Reference 6.1

▶ *In the following sentences choose the correct pronouns and write them in the blanks at the right.*

EXAMPLE

The Texas Rangers patrol the vast Texas plains as (they, it, one) did a century ago.   *they*

1. Model railroad enthusiasts, (who, which) numbered in the hundreds, took a trip from Durango to Silverton, Colorado, on the narrow-gauge railway.   _____

2. The German immigrants to the United States (who, which) came here in the last hundred years have added much to America's culture.   _____

3. The first-graders in Mr. Philips' class built a small house out of cardboard for (one's, their) project.   _____

4. Many of the early prospectors for gold in California found (theirselves, themselves) penniless and had to work for their grubstake.   _____

5. Not only the governor but also the legislators know that (he, she, they) must answer to the voters.   _____

6. Keeping (its, their) budget under control, the company was able to save several thousand dollars.   _____

7. Dana Morey and her assistants are turning (her, their) attention to more radical architectural designs.   _____

8. People who swim without supervision endanger (one's life, their lives).   _____

9. Large corporations in the United States (who, which) do international business value college graduates with a knowledge of foreign languages. _____

10. Many researchers are now studying the causes of failure to find ways to prevent (it, them). _____

Copyright © 1982 by Houghton Mifflin Company

Pronouns: Agreement and Reference   6.2

▶ *In the following sentences choose the correct pronouns and write them in the blanks at the right.*

EXAMPLE

(Who, Whom) answered the door?

$$\underline{\textit{Who}}$$

(subject of verb *answered*)

1. The researchers working on sleep deprivation reported that (his or her, their) subjects became paranoid after several days without sleep.

   _____

2. Laying bricks takes patience and skill; (it requires, they require) a long apprenticeship.

   _____

3. The women's basketball team from our school won (its, their) division title.

   _____

4. The well drillers finally found water at 700 feet, the lowest depth (it, they) had ever had to drill.

   _____

5. The club made enough money with (its, their) booksale to provide six scholarships.

   _____

6. Children often have imaginary friends to whom (they are, he is) especially attached.

   _____

7. The students discussed the issue with animation—some of (them, it), with outright hostility.

   _____

8. Because Ramon was the best of carpenters, few of the customers were dissatisfied with (his, their) work.

   _____

9. After Mr. Kovic finished reading his poems, some members of the audience rose from (its, their) seats and applauded.

   _____

10. The media were at the royal wedding in great numbers with (their, its) cameras, notebooks, and microphones.

   _____

Copyright © 1982 by Houghton Mifflin Company

Case   6.3

▶ *Write the correct case form in the following sentences in the blanks at the right.*

EXAMPLE

(Whoever, Whomever) invented the wheel deserves the *Whoever*
gratitude of everyone.   (subject of verb *invented*)

1. The coaches decided (who, whom) to select as player of the year.

    _____

2. The bush pilot and (I, me) drank hot coffee while we flew over the frozen tundra.

    _____

3. I cannot recall (me, my) behaving rudely at the party.

    _____

4. At the end, the watermelon-eating contest was between (she, her) and (I, me).

    _____

5. Two members of the club—Sherri and (I, me)— were asked to decorate the registration booth.

    _____

6. (He, His) running the red light almost caused an accident.

    _____

7. No typist in the class can type as rapidly as (he, him).

    _____

8. The band members asked (themselves, theirselves) what had gone wrong during the rehearsal.

    _____

9. We knew (her, she) to be loyal to her principles.

    _____

10. He dedicated his book to (whoever, whomever) cherished liberty.

    _____

Copyright © 1982 by Houghton Mifflin Company

Case 6.4

▶ *Write the correct case form in the following sentences in the blanks at the right.*

EXAMPLE

(Their, Them) singing is delightful.

Their

(possessive case with gerund)

1. (Us, We) office managers attended a seminar on motivation.

   _____

2. The oboe player told (I, me, myself) that he had been playing since he was six years old.

   _____

3. For (me, I) to enjoy a movie, I must have a candy bar and popcorn.

   _____

4. Skydiving was a thrilling experience for Mary, (I, me), and the other novices.

   _____

5. When I saw that my sister had so much work to do, I offered to divide the jobs evenly between (she, her) and me.

   _____

6. (Who, Whom) did the publisher decide to choose as the new editor?

   _____

7. Many Americans complain that (we, us) taxpayers must pay too much money to the government.

   _____

8. We helped more than (they, them), but they received more credit.

   _____

9. The governor traveled to France with my wife and (I, me) to celebrate Bastille Day.

   _____

10. (Whoever, Whomever) owns the disputed land near the present borders of Wyoming and Colorado may be wealthy some day.

   _____

Copyright © 1982 by Houghton Mifflin Company

NAME _____

DATE _____ SCORE _____

Case 6.5

▶ *Write the correct case form in the following sentences in the blank at the right.*

EXAMPLE

The champions were Doug and (I, me).　　　　　_____I_____

1. The new clerk at the post office likes to help people start stamp collections and finds (they, them) interested in the new hobby.　　　_____

2. "We have a problem before us, and (us, we) must find a quick answer," the captain stated.　　_____

3. More people came to the reception than any of (we, us) expected.　　_____

4. The candy was evenly divided between you and (I, me).　　_____

5. The actress thought nò one was as pretty as (she, her).　　_____

6. Everyone was pleased at (him, his) coming to the party.　　_____

7. The chef said, "It is (I, me) who baked the bread."　　_____

8. When the investigation of the fire began, the experts were able to determine (who, whom) caused it.　　_____

9. "Can anyone tell me (who, whom) our twenty-third president was?" the historian asked.　　_____

10. "The last of (we, us) to leave should lock the doors," the librarian said.　　_____

Adjectives and adverbs compared

Adjectives modify nouns and pronouns. **Adverbs** modify verbs, adjectives, and other adverbs.

The bright light hurt *our* eyes. (*The* and *bright* are adjectives modifying *light,* and *our* is a possessive adjective modifying *eyes.*)

The news spread *quickly.* (*Quickly* is an adverb modifying *spread.*)

Most adverbs end in *-ly.* Only a few adjectives (*lovely, friendly,* for example) have this ending. Some adverbs have two forms, one with *-ly* and one without (*closely, close* and *quickly, quick*). Most adverbs are formed by adding *-ly* to adjectives (*sudden, suddenly* and *hasty, hastily.*)

We had an *easy* choice to make. (*Easy* is an adjective.)

We made the choice *easily.* (*Easily* is an adverb.)

Use a predicate adjective, not an adverb, after a linking verb, such as *be, become, seem, look, appear, feel, sound, smell, taste.*

The *meat* tastes *bad.* (*Bad* describes the *meat.*)

The *actress* felt *calm.* (*Calm* describes the *actress.*)

One feels *good* after finishing a long swim. (*Good* describes how one feels.)

BUT

After treatment, the patient feels *well.* (Adverb *well* describes a state of health.)

Forms of the comparative and superlative

Use the **comparative form** of the adjective to refer to two things; use the **superlative form** to refer to more than two. Add *-er* or *-est* to form the comparative and the superlative of most short modifiers.

The new air terminal is much *larger* than the old one.

Of the five hotels in our city, the *newest* one is the *largest.*

Use *more* or *most* (or *less* or *least*) rather than *-er* and *-est* before long modifiers, that is, modifiers of several syllables.

He is *more capable* than his brother. (not *capabler*)

He is the *most capable* person I know. (not *capablest*)

He is very *fast.* (predicate adjective)

He is *faster* than his brother. (comparative form)

He is the *fastest* runner in our class. (superlative form)

Some adjectives and adverbs have irregular comparative and superlative forms:

good, better, best: bad, worse, worst

    Copyright © 1982 by Houghton Mifflin Company

Adjective or Adverb?   7.1

▶ *Write the correct form of adjective or adverb in the blank at the right.*

EXAMPLE

A (high, highly) productive honeybee hive is fascinating.   *highly*

(adverb *highly* modifies adjective *productive*)

1. (Appropriate, Appropriately) dress is requested by the restaurant.   _____
2. Graduates (enthusiastic, enthusiastically) threw their caps into the air.   _____
3. Trains must travel (slow, slowly) within city limits.   _____
4. The review included a (remarkable, remarkably) accurate account of the complicated plot.   _____
5. Telephone costs to consumers in real dollars are (considerable, considerably) less than they were a few years ago.   _____
6. After deciding which college to attend, she felt (good, well) about her decision.   _____
7. Every applicant performed (good, well) in the tests.   _____
8. Mail may be delayed (frequent, frequently) by bad weather.   _____
9. The plain before the pioneers was (vast, vastly) and covered with wildflowers.   _____
10. (Really, Real) good ice cream is now available in over fifty flavors and at a reasonable cost.   _____
11. Teams that remain (close, closely) are usually very successful.   _____
12. The fresh cookies went (quick, quickly).   _____
13. The newscaster told the anxious audience that the rescue was going as (good, well) as could be expected.   _____
14. The Western Hemisphere has two of the world's (larger, largest) rivers, the Amazon and the Mississippi; of the two, the Amazon is the (larger, largest), but the Mississippi is the (most, more) important economically.   _____
15. Once on the endangered species list, the American alligator is now (abundant, abundantly) be-

cause of (more strict, stricter) law enforcement
and better game management. _____
16. The economists found it was not (possible, possibly) for them to predict interest rates. _____
17. Of all the space walks, Armstrong's was the (better, best). _____
18. The stock cars passed the stands so (rapidly,
rapid) that it was impossible to tell (accurate, accurately) who was ahead. _____
19. Being (solid, solidly) behind the new housing
program, the young politicians had to fight opponents who were (strong, strongly) opposed to
them. _____
20. Most conductors are (kind of, somewhat) pleased
with requests for encores. _____

   Copyright © 1982 by Houghton Mifflin Company

Adjective or Adverb?   7.2

▶ *Write the correct forms of adjectives or adverbs in the blanks at the right.*

EXAMPLE

The cake looks (good, well).

good

(adjective *good* after linking verb)

1. The grizzly bear is the (more, most) unpredictable of the bear species. _____

2. Of all the memorials in Washington, D.C., the Lincoln Memorial is the (more, most) visited. _____

3. The secret agent uncovered a (close, closely) guarded secret. _____

4. The people looked (sad, sadly) as the workmen started demolishing the oldest school in town. _____

5. "Each word in your essays must be spelled (correct, correctly)," the instructor warned. _____

6. Trent tried to complete his homework as (quick, quickly) as possible. _____

7. "If you want a (real, really) effective stereo that plays music (clear, clearly)," the clerk advised, "we'll sell you a graphic equalizer." _____

8. After the relay race, the losing team looked (kind of, somewhat) (glum, glumly) and said that they felt (worse, worst, worser, badder) than they looked. _____

9. As the cowboy (careful, carefully) put his cup of very thick coffee down, he remarked to the waitress, "One thing about your coffee: it sure ain't scared." _____

10. Because the waitress scowled, the cowboy became more (careful, carefully) when he spoke. _____

Copyright © 1982 by Houghton Mifflin Company

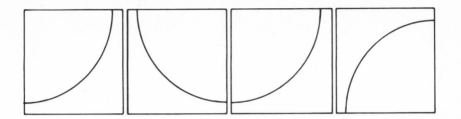

Sentence Structure

Choppy Sentences and Excessive Coordination 8

Linking a number of short dependent clauses and sentences produces wordiness and monotony and fails to show precise relationships between thoughts.

EXAMPLE

The United States has changed significantly in the last fifty years, for the life expectancy of Americans has increased ten years for men and fifteen years for women, and the nation's work force has quadrupled.

IMPROVED

The United States has changed significantly in the last fifty years. The life expectancy of Americans has increased ten years for men and fifteen years for women. In addition, the nation's work force has quadrupled.

Subordination

Use subordinate clauses accurately and effectively to avoid excessive coordination and to achieve variety and emphasis. However, avoid excessive subordination, which may ruin style or create excessively long sentences.

EXCESSIVE SUBORDINATION

My grandfather took great pleasure throughout his life in the craft of carving wooden figures, which he learned to do when he was young, which was a time when people did not have the great number of amusements which we have today.

BETTER

My grandfather, who lived in a time when people did not have the great number of amusements of today, learned when young to carve wooden figures. He took great pleasure in the craft throughout his life.

Express main ideas in independent clauses; express less important ideas in subordinate clauses.

IMPROPER SUBORDINATION

Few people know that he got his seed from mills that made apple cider, although Johnny Appleseed became famous for planting apple trees throughout the Ohio Valley.

BETTER

Although Johnny Appleseed became famous for planting apple trees throughout the Ohio Valley, few people know that he got his seed from mills that made apple cider.

Copyright © 1982 by Houghton Mifflin Company

Avoid excessive overlapping of subordinate clauses. A series of clauses with each one depending on the previous one is confusing.

OVERLAPPING SUBORDINATION
The United States Treasury Department, which is located in Washington, which is responsible for the printing and minting of currency, is also responsible for the protection of the President.

IMPROVED
Located in Washington, the United States Treasury Department is responsible for the printing and minting of currency and for the protection of the President.

Completeness
After *so, such, too*
Make your sentences complete in structure and thought, especially sentences with *so, such,* and *too.*

NOT CLEAR
The house was so hot. (so hot that something must have happened)

CLEAR
The house was so hot that we had to turn on the air conditioner.

NOT CLEAR
The room was in such confusion. (What happened?)

CLEAR
The room was in such confusion that we could not find the telephone book.

Omission of verbs and prepositions
Do not omit a verb or a preposition that is necessary to the structure of the sentence.

NOT
We were interested and then bored by the lecture.

BUT
We were interested in and then bored by the lecture.

NOT
The passengers were impatient and the plane late.

BUT
The passengers were impatient, and the plane was late.

Omission of *that*
The omission of *that* is often confusing.

INCOMPLETE

The museum said the painting was a forgery.

COMPLETE

The museum said that the painting was a forgery.

Comparisons

Make comparisons clear and complete by comparing only similar terms, using the word *other* where necessary, and avoiding awkward and incomplete comparisons.

INCORRECT

The bite of a great white shark is worse than a snake.

LOGICAL

The bite of a great white shark is worse than the bite of a snake.

INCORRECT

The Grand Canyon is larger than any canyon in the world.

LOGICAL

The Grand Canyon is larger than any other canyon in the world.

INCORRECT

Reading is one of the most pleasant if not the most pleasant pastime one can enjoy. (After *one of the most pleasant,* the plural *pastimes* is required.)

BETTER

Reading is one of the most pleasant pastimes one can enjoy, if not the most pleasant.

OR

Reading is one of the most pleasant pastimes.

Avoid ambiguous comparisons.

AMBIGUOUS

We enjoyed visiting the city more than our parents. (*More* than visiting parents, or *more* than the parents enjoyed the city?)

CLEAR

We enjoyed visiting the city more than our parents did.

Consistency

Avoid confusing shifts in grammatical forms.

 Copyright © 1982 by Houghton Mifflin Company

Shifts in tense

INCORRECT
The doctor was well trained, but his patients are dissatisfied.

CORRECT
The doctor is well trained, but his patients are dissatisfied.

Shifts in person

INCORRECT
When we left our hotel, you could see the capitol building.

CORRECT
When we left our hotel, we could see the capitol building.

Shifts in number

INCORRECT
A person may cheat on his income taxes, and then they deny it.

CORRECT
People cheat on their income taxes, and then they deny it.

Shifts in voice

INCORRECT
The assignment *is read* by the student, and then she *answers* the questions at the end of the chapter. (Put both parts of the sentence in the active voice.)

CORRECT
The student *reads* the assignment, and then she *answers* the questions at the end of the chapter.

Copyright © 1982 by Houghton Mifflin Company

Excessive Coordination   8.1

Sentences should be varied in length, structure, and emphasis. Coordination, subordination, parallelism, and word order show relationships precisely and emphasize important elements of thought. Do not string together a number of short independent clauses; excessive coordination fails to show precise relationships between thoughts.

▶ *Rewrite the following sentences to eliminate excessive coordination.*

EXAMPLE

The election results are close and both candidates declared victory, so the officials decided to recount the ballots.

Because the election results were close and both candidates declared victory, the officials decided to recount the ballots.

1. Uncle John liked to gossip and he was the local barber and he lived in the small town of Sheffield, Colorado.

   _____

   _____

   _____

   _____

2. The visitors were foreign, and they had an exciting day in San Francisco, and they visited Fisherman's Wharf, Alcatraz, and Golden Gate Park.

   _____

   _____

   _____

   _____

3. Many of the great movies of the 1930s and earlier have been remade

one or more times, and these include *Ben Hur, The Champ, Romeo and Juliet,* and *King Kong.*

_____

_____

_____

_____

4. The University of Georgia was the first land-grant college, and it was established in 1785, and the town near it was named Athens, and that was the name of the ancient Greek center of civilization.

_____

_____

_____

_____

5. With the current shortage of energy and minerals, geology is becoming increasingly important, and it is the study of the structure of rocks and the history of the earth.

_____

_____

_____

_____

6. The old-fashioned fairy tales were frightening, and they were intended to be, and children heard them and were likely to stay on the path in the woods or near home, so the stories taught safety.

_____

_____

_____

_____

7. The bazooka was an antitank weapon, and it was developed during World War II, but its name came from an odd musical instrument that was created by a popular comedian of the 1940s.

_____

_____

  Copyright © 1982 by Houghton Mifflin Company

_____

_____

8. Sun spots have remained a mystery for two centuries, and they were discovered in the eighteenth century, but now scientists are beginning to understand these solar phenomena.

_____

_____

_____

_____

9. Some parents do not listen to their children, and they do not encourage them to talk; consequently, their children are not easily able to express verbally their fears, and they cannot talk about their hostilities.

_____

_____

_____

_____

10. The Tasaday were discovered recently, and they live in a remote area of the Philippines, and, moreover, they are living examples of Stone Age people.

_____

_____

_____

_____

Copyright © 1982 by Houghton Mifflin Company

Subordination 8.2

▶ *Indicate which sentence in each of the following pairs is preferable because the writer either uses correct subordination or eliminates excessive coordination.*

EXAMPLE

_*a.*_ a. In the Southwest one can visit prehistoric cliff dwellings, which were built into canyon walls.
    b. In the Southwest one can visit, which were built into canyon walls, prehistoric cliff dwellings.

_____ 1. a. The Siamese cats were in trouble, and they broke a precious lamp.
    b. When they broke a precious lamp, the Siamese cats were in trouble.

_____ 2. a. When its seeds are sown by the winds that blow across the prairie, the tumbleweed dries and breaks from its roots.
    b. When the tumbleweed dries and breaks from its roots, its seed are sown by the winds that blow across the prairie.

_____ 3. a. The drought is severe, and the nation will avoid food shortages through imports, but it will need rain for late crops.
    b. Although the nation will avoid food shortages through imports, the drought is severe, and rain is needed for late crops.

_____ 4. a. The balloonists began their attempt to cross the continent, and they generally had good weather, but the winds became unfavorable.
    b. When the balloonists began their attempt to cross the continent, they had good weather, but the winds became unfavorable.

_____ 5. a. The *Mayflower,* which brought the Pilgrims to the New World, smelled sweet because it often had been used to transport wine.
    b. The *Mayflower* brought the Pilgrims to the New World, and it smelled sweet because it often had been used to transport wine.

_____ 6. a. Apple pie has been more popular since the end of the eighteenth century, although pumpkin pie was served a century earlier.

    b. Although pumpkin pie was served a century earlier, apple pie has been more popular since the end of the eighteenth century.

_____ 7. a. In 1803 Thomas Jefferson purchased the Louisiana Territory which contained over fifty million acres of hardwood forest that has now been reduced to three and one-half million acres.

    b. When Thomas Jefferson purchased the Louisiana Territory in 1803, it contained over fifty million acres of hardwood forest, which has now been reduced to three and one-half million acres.

_____ 8. a. The Center for Disease Control is a federal agency, and it has the responsibility to diagnose and trace the sources of infectious diseases, and it is located in Atlanta, Georgia.

    b. The Center for Disease Control, which is responsible for diagnosing and tracing the sources of infectious diseases, is located in Atlanta, Georgia.

_____ 9. a. The store manager had discussed several changes in company policy, and he asked for questions, and then he listened intently to what the employees said.

    b. After the store manager had discussed several changes in company policy and asked for questions, he then listened intently to what the employees said.

_____10. a. The first gold rush took place in Dahlonega, Georgia, in 1828, but there have been many gold rushes in the United States, and some have had greater historical impact.

    b. Although there have been many gold rushes in the United States of greater historical impact, the first one took place in Dahlonega, Georgia, in 1828.

     Copyright © 1982 by Houghton Mifflin Company

NAME _____

DATE _____ SCORE _____

Subordination 8.3

▶ *Revise the following sentences to achieve effective subordination.*

EXAMPLE

The last of our campaign funds were almost gone, and this caused the cancelation of most of the television advertisements.

When our campaign funds were almost gone, most of the Television advertisements had to be canceled.

1. The storm grew in strength, and the people became frightened.

   _____

   _____

   _____

2. Registered voters should participate in every election and they can expect public officials to be responsive to their views.

   _____

   _____

   _____

3. The Weather Bureau and the Coast Guard issue small-craft warnings when storms are likely, and small craft should return to port.

   _____

   _____

   _____

4. The worst tornado in the United States struck Missouri, Illinois, and Indiana in 1925, and nearly seven hundred people lost their lives.

   _____

   _____

   _____

5. The Girl's Club added a new wing to its building and will be able to accommodate five hundred new members and include many new programs.

_____

_____

_____

6. Elaine was an industrious employee who was soon to be promoted to a position in management and who was studying accounting at a local college.

_____

_____

_____

7. Many people did not understand the meaning of such terms as "head of household" and "parochial" on the 1970 census form, and the 1980 census form contained many simpler terms.

_____

_____

_____

8. Many Americans take their vacations in the early spring, and this way they avoid the heavy winter rains and the dry summer months.

_____

_____

_____

9. Flamingos are large birds which wade in search of food and have red or pink plumage and have long legs, long necks, and a bill that turns downward at the tip.

_____

_____

_____

10. A justice of the peace is a magistrate at the lowest level of a state's court system who performs marriages, who administers oaths, and

Copyright © 1982 by Houghton Mifflin Company

who usually acts upon minor offenses that otherwise would crowd the dockets of higher courts.

_____

_____

_____

Copyright © 1982 by Houghton Mifflin Company

Completeness and Comparisons 8.4

▶ *Revise the following sentences to correct any errors in completeness and comparisons.*

EXAMPLES

The colonel was too old.

The colonel was too old to be an astronaut.

Rafting on the Colorado River is more exciting than any river in the United States.

Rafting on the Colorado River is more exciting than rafting on any other river in the United States.

1. Polls are often so inaccurate.

   _____

   _____

2. Modern jetliners are different.

   _____

   _____

3. Sometimes the pace of a football game seems slower.

   _____

   _____

4. Many insects are as small if not smaller than the head of a pin.

   _____

   _____

5. During the baseball season more people supported the local team.

   _____

   _____

6. Forgetting a school assignment is worse than any mistake in school.

   _____

   _____

7. The tenant in the apartment was both interested and suspicious of his neighbor.

   _____

   _____

8. The new investigative reporter was as good if not better than some of the older reporters.

   _____

   _____

9. The new play at the Helen Hayes Theater is one of the most interesting if not the most interesting play this season.

   _____

   _____

10. My boyfriend liked me better than my friend Jane.

   _____

   _____

Copyright © 1982 by Houghton Mifflin Company

Completeness and Comparisons 8.5

▶ *Revise the following sentences to correct any errors in completeness and comparisons.*

EXAMPLE

No one works harder.

No one works harder than John.

1. The substitute announcer speaks faster.

2. Racquetball is almost as popular.

3. Many children understand their personal problems better.

4. A completely rebuilt engine is usually just as dependable.

5. Commercial television is more interesting and less beneficial.

6. Fluorescent light is as cheap if not cheaper than any other commercial lighting system.

7. Her speech was as clear as if not clearer than any she had made in the past.

8. The new business regulations are both examples and guides to the administration's traditional economic policies.

_____

_____

9. The clerk had never and never would be eligible for a long vacation because he took so many days off during the year.

_____

_____

10. Sri Lanka, formerly Ceylon, has and continues to be the world's chief supplier of natural cinnamon.

_____

_____

Copyright © 1982 by Houghton Mifflin Company

Consistency 8.6

▶ *Revise the following sentences making them structurally consistent. Avoid unnecessary shifts in tense, person, mood, or voice and shifts from one relative pronoun to another.*

EXAMPLE

Abraham Lincoln was only fifty-two when he becomes the sixteenth President of the United States.

Abraham Lincoln was only fifty-two when he became the sixteenth President of the United States.

1. I enjoy a cold glass of iced tea because one feels refreshed after you drink it.

_____

_____

2. Each of you have been given complete instructions, so one should not make any mistakes.

_____

_____

3. Every box has been wrapped carefully so it had not come open in the mail.

_____

_____

4. Charles Levinson started the project, but it was not completed by him.

_____

_____

5. Because many buses have broken down this week, people were having to drive to work.

_____

_____

INSTRUCTIONAL SERVICE CENTER

6. When they were in school, they are busy in many clubs.

_____

_____

7. The woman discovered the real identity of her friend after she knows her for twenty years.

_____

_____

8. After we had been hiking for several days, we grow tired and stop to rest.

_____

_____

9. One of my closest friends was Larry Marconi, who is my neighbor.

_____

_____

10. We went to a dance that I and he thoroughly enjoyed.

_____

_____

Copyright © 1982 by Houghton Mifflin Company

Position of Modifiers, Parallelism, Sentence Variety 9

Modifiers

Attach modifiers to the correct word or element in the sentence to avoid confusion. Most adjectives precede the noun they modify. Adverbs may come before or follow the words they modify. Prepositional phrases usually follow the word they modify, as do adjective clauses. Adverbial phrases and clauses may be placed in various positions—as decided by the writer.

EXAMPLES

The new tests are finished. (adjectives before the noun)

The new tests *soon* ended. (adverb before the verb)

The new tests ended *soon*. (adverb after the verb)

The man *on the corner* hailed a cab. (prepositional phrase modifying *man*)

The man came *to the door*. (prepositional phrase modifying *came*)

Sooner than we expected, the movie ended. (adverbial clause modifying *ended*)

The movie ended *sooner than we expected*. (adverbial clause modifying *ended*)

Dangling modifiers

Avoid dangling modifiers. A verbal phrase at the beginning of a sentence should modify the subject of the sentence.

Dangling participle

Seeing the fresh apple pie, *my hunger* grew.

CLEAR

Seeing the fresh apple pie, *I* grew hungry.

Dangling gerund

After examining my checkbook, *my error* was found.

CLEAR

After examining my checkbook, *I found* my error.

Dangling infinitive

To get an early start, *the alarm clock* was set for 6 A.M.

CLEAR

To get an early start, *I set* the alarm clock for 6 A.M.

Dangling prepositional phrase

While *in school,* my mother did her shopping.

CORRECT

While *I was* in school, my mother did her shopping.

Misplaced modifiers, squinting modifiers

Almost any modifier that comes between an adjective clause and the word it modifies can cause confusion.

UNCLEAR

Many people are released by the courts *who may be guilty.*

CLEAR

Many people *who may be guilty* are released by the courts.

A modifier placed between two words so that it may modify either word is a **squinting modifier.**

UNCLEAR

The chess master who was playing *carefully* won the first game.

CLEAR

The chess master who was *carefully* playing won the first game.

Separation of elements

Do not separate closely related elements, such as the subject and the verb, parts of a verb phrase, or a verb and an object.

AWKWARD

The construction workers *had,* for the last week, *expected* a new contract.

IMPROVED

For the last week, the construction workers *had expected* a new contract.

Avoid **split infinitives** (modifiers between *to* and the verb form).

NOT

to actively *pursue*

BUT

to pursue actively

Parallelism

Make construction in a sentence parallel (balanced) by matching phrase with phrase, clause with clause, verb with verb, and so on.

 Copyright © 1982 by Houghton Mifflin Company

The men argued *bitterly* and *were loud.*

The men argued *bitterly* and *loudly.*

Repeat an article *(a, an,* or *the)*, a preposition *(by, in, for,* and so on), or other words to preserve parallelism and clarity.

The aircraft was *in a storm* and *trouble.*

The aircraft was *in the storm* and *in trouble.*

Sentence variety

Vary sentences in structure and order. Use loose, periodic, and balanced sentence forms.

A **loose sentence** makes its main point at the beginning of the sentence and then adds qualifications or refinements.

We left early, missing the heavy traffic.

A **periodic sentence** saves the main point until the end of a sentence to create suspense or emphasis.

After a long afternoon visiting my aunt, I was eager to go home.

A **balanced sentence** has parallel parts in terms of structure, length, and thoughts.

We must work so that we may live, not live that we may work.

Copyright © 1982 by Houghton Mifflin Company

Position of Modifiers   9.1

▶ *Revise the following sentences to correct faulty modifiers.*

1. Dieting suddenly increases your appetite.

   _____

   _____

2. Most fishermen catch fish with skill and patience.

   _____

   _____

3. The pilot saved the jetliner using an emergency landing strip.

   _____

   _____

4. Hoping to increase sales, credit policies were changed by the store owners.

   _____

   _____

5. People who can do difficult tasks easily find themselves with more than they can do.

   _____

   _____

6. Suddenly reaching an arm through the bars of the cage, the man's pocket was torn by the monkey.

   _____

   _____

7. The motorcyclist turned sharply right effortlessly missing the barrier on the race track.

   _____

   _____

8. At the crossing the train passed by the auto pulling fifty boxcars and a caboose.

   _____

   _____

9. Pedestrians stepped in the cement walking across the new sidewalk.

   _____

   _____

10. The band marched down the street proudly showing off their new uniforms.

    _____

    _____

Copyright © 1982 by Houghton Mifflin Company

Position of Modifiers 9.2

▶ *Revise the following sentences to correct faulty modifiers.*

1. Reaching into the canoe, the camera fell into the swift current.

   _____

   _____

2. He bought a pickup truck from a friend with a camper top.

   _____

   _____

3. Going to the mountains occasionally pleases Trent and his family.

   _____

   _____

4. People can hear Americans who speak Gullah, an English dialect, visiting the South Carolina and Georgia coasts.

   _____

   _____

5. With two additional secretaries, the judge's crowded days were made easier.

   _____

   _____

6. Receiving a substantial raise, the worker's house could be repaired.

   _____

   _____

7. The secretary typed the letter using the office's newest electric typewriter.

   _____

   _____

8. At a dance only once Patricia was embarrassed.

   _____

   _____

9. Television stations that run too many old movies frequently lose viewers.

   _____

   _____

10. Using profanity often hurts oneself rather than others.

   _____

   _____

Copyright © 1982 by Houghton Mifflin Company

Separation of Elements   9.3

▶ *Do not unnecessarily separate closely related elements. Separation of parts of a verb phrase, a verb and its object, or a subject and its verb can be awkward or misleading. Revise the following sentences by correcting unnecessarily separated elements.*

EXAMPLE

The domestication of animals had, years before civilization began, become commonplace in Egypt.

The domestication of animals had become commonplace in Egypt years before civilization began.

1. The traffic controller, especially tired from working his difficult shift, stopped by the cafeteria to have coffee.

   _____

   _____

2. The boys have, since they met in the first grade at St. John Elementary School, been the best of friends.

   _____

   _____

3. Mabel has always succeeded, as long as anyone can remember, in making others happy.

   _____

   _____

4. Shoppers who read the advertisements in newspapers may find, if they search carefully, real bargains.

   _____

   _____

5. Marvin, after he had spent the afternoon looking for old bottles at the city dump, took his discoveries home to add to his collection.

   _____

   _____

6. People always need to, whenever they plan a trip, make certain the police are notified that they will be away from home.

_____

_____

7. Eating in new restaurants, although it is sometimes a great mistake, is usually quite exciting.

_____

_____

8. Maria, using the money she had earned as a clinical psychologist, bought the stereo equipment she had wanted for several years.

_____

_____

9. Micah watched, through the living-room window, with envy as his older brother and sister left for the first day of school.

_____

_____

10. There was hope that Nicole, although she had not received any information, would hear about her scholarship in a few days.

_____

_____

Copyright © 1982 by Houghton Mifflin Company

Parallelism 9.4

▶ *Revise the following sentences to correct faulty parallelism.*

EXAMPLE

At the heart of Romanticism are individuality, a pantheistic view of nature, and organicism.

At the heart of Romanticism are individualism, pantheism, and organicism.

1. The man was neither for the new taxes or against them.

   _____

   _____

2. The accountant spent the morning calling clients and balanced their books.

   _____

   _____

3. The driver raced into town and driving to the center of the business district.

   _____

   _____

4. Political campaigning would be difficult for a shy person or if one disliked traveling.

   _____

   _____

5. The clown was laughing and ate her ice-cream cone at the same time.

   _____

   _____

6. Travelers crossing southern Texas pass through Beaumont, Houston, San Antonio, and then they drive to El Paso.

_____

_____

7. The attorney advised her client to testify in his own behalf and against taking the Fifth Amendment.

_____

_____

8. At school he found that he hated eating in the cafeteria, studying for his chemistry class, and laundry.

_____

_____

9. After shopping at the department store, the two friends visited an art gallery and then were watching a movie.

_____

_____

10. Although the fire inside the cabin was warm, the air was damp, the walls were cold, and the wind whispering through the cracks near the windows.

_____

_____

Copyright © 1982 by Houghton Mifflin Company

Parallelism 9.5

▶ *Revise the following sentences to correct faulty parallelism.*

EXAMPLE

The soprano sang with a pure tone and beautifully.

The soprano sang with purity and beauty.

1. The weather reporter predicted rain and that it would not last all day.

   _____

   _____

2. The timid soul was afraid of dogs and cats terrified him.

   _____

   _____

3. The singer's voice was magnificent, and the crowd applauds her.

   _____

   _____

4. Either one studies now or it will fail one later.

   _____

   _____

5. Camping is great fun if one is not bothered by the fleas, ticks, mosquitoes, and their bites.

   _____

   _____

6. To renew one's spirit, to test one's endurance, and feel at peace with nature—these are the benefits of survival hikes.

   _____

   _____

7. Our vacation will be a success if we visit Carlsbad Caverns, the White Sands National Park, and that we will see Yellowstone Park.

   _____

8. The contractor opposed the scientists' request that he delay construction and excavating the archeological site.

_____

_____

9. The Treasury Department scrutinized all the amendments to the tax bills for unintentional loopholes, typographical errors, and to see if they contained windfall tax credits for special interests.

_____

_____

_____

10. Pine trees are the most profitable investment for the forest-products industry; they grow fast, they provide lumber as well as pulp, and naval stores such as turpentines and resins are their by-products.

_____

_____

_____

_____

Copyright © 1982 by Houghton Mifflin Company

Variety in Sentences 9.6

▶ *Make one sentence out of each of the groups below. Vary your sentences in length, structure, and order. Write simple, compound, and complex patterns, and vary your sentences between loose, periodic, and balanced forms. A loose sentence, the most frequent kind, makes the main point early and then adds refinements. A periodic sentence withholds an element of the main thought until the end and thus creates suspense and emphasis. A balanced sentence has parts which are similar in structure and length and which express parallel thoughts.*

EXAMPLE

J.D. Salinger is a novelist.
He is an eccentric recluse.
His most famous novel is *The Catcher in the Rye*.

Novelist J. D. Salinger, whose most famous novel is The Catcher in the Rye, is an eccentric recluse.

1. Sawdust is not a waste product.
   It is a main ingredient of particle board.
   Some furniture is made of particle board.

   _____

   _____

   _____

   _____

2. Latex paint has a water base.
   It dries faster than oil-base paint.
   It resists moisture.

   _____

   _____

   _____

   _____

3. Most primitive societies have traditional stories.
   These stories tell of heroes on journeys.
   Some of them are called myths.

   _____

   _____

   _____

   _____

4. Ice cream is a very old dessert.
   Romans brought ice from the mountains of northern Italy.
   They mixed the ice with cream and honey.

   _____

   _____

   _____

   _____

5. Clothing made of synthetic materials has been popular since World
      War II.
   Cotton is becoming popular again.
   Cotton fabric that will hold a permanent press can now be manufac-
      tured.

   _____

   _____

   _____

   _____

6. Termites do considerable damage.
   Homeowners may suspect the presence of termites if they see large
      red ants, which are called carpenter ants.
   These ants eat termites.

   _____

   _____

   _____

   _____

7. Detroit is now making a light automobile.
   Light automobiles use less fuel.

Copyright © 1982 by Houghton Mifflin Company

Some do less damage to highway surfaces than do large cars.
Many see these cars as an economic necessity.

_____

_____

_____

_____

8. The costs of owning a swimming pool are greater than initial construction expenses.
Pools must be routinely maintained.
Additional liability insurance is a necessity for the swimming-pool owner.

_____

_____

_____

_____

9. Soft contact lenses are quite popular.
They require more care than hard contact lenses do.
The lenses must be washed daily and cleaned with a special solution once a month.

_____

_____

_____

_____

10. Columbus is supposed to have discovered America in the fifteenth century.
Norsemen are credited with discovering the New World around 1000 A.D.
The first people to find the New World probably crossed a land bridge between Siberia and Alaska between 18,000 and 14,000 B.C.

_____

_____

_____

_____

Copyright © 1982 by Houghton Mifflin Company

Variety in Sentences   9.7

▶ *Revise the following sentences for greatest emphasis and for the most logical or climactic order. Write C to the left of any correct sentence.*

EXAMPLE

On the legislative agenda are tax reform, billboard regulations, and new committee assignments.

On the legislative agenda are new committee assignments, billboard regulations, and tax reform.

(Revised to move from least to most important item.)

1. She won the women's amateur tennis championship six years after she started competition in the city tournaments.

   _____

   _____

   _____

2. An alligator devoured the fish on the stringer as the fisherman was tying up his boat.

   _____

   _____

   _____

3. The runner broke his best time, beat his opponents in the meet, and set a world record.

   _____

   _____

   _____

4. The earthquake destroyed an entire section of the city, interrupted communications, and damaged several highways.

   _____

   _____

5. The famous novelist toured several countries, won the Nobel Prize, and finished his twentieth book.

_____

_____

_____

6. When she broke her watch, she was upset and tried to find the pieces.

_____

_____

_____

7. After the machinist lost his position, he was interviewed by several companies, searched the want advertising for a new job, and wrote letters listing his qualifications.

_____

_____

_____

_____

8. Both political candidates have previous public service; they have served in the United States Senate, on the state board of mines, and on the local school board.

_____

_____

_____

_____

9. The department store's Christmas tree was crowned with a magnificent silver star, surrounded by dozens of gifts covered with gold paper, decorated with hundreds of red ornaments and lights.

_____

_____

_____

_____

Copyright © 1982 by Houghton Mifflin Company

10. Using a metal detector for the first time, the beachcombers found discarded soft-drink cans, an expensive gold bracelet, and silver coins.

_____

_____

_____

_____

Copyright © 1982 by Houghton Mifflin Company

Variety in Sentences   9.8

▶ *Identify the following sentences as loose or periodic.*

EXAMPLE

After many years of failure, the old miner struck gold.   *periodic*

The old miner struck gold after many years of failure.   *loose*

1. Although some people think that success in school is a good indication of success in later life, surveys of people who have become successful show little or no relationship between the two.   _____

2. The animals moved to higher ground when water from the flooding river reached them.   _____

3. Although the city routinely sprayed every neighborhood and nearby swamps, the mosquitoes continued to swarm.   _____

4. Flash floods hit the desert when several inches of rain fell during a single day.   _____

5. The coral snake can be deadly, although it is marked by beautiful red, yellow, and black bands.   _____

6. Many of the sailors began to shout when their ship reached landfall and they could see their home port again.   _____

7. The group visited the Lincoln Memorial on the last day of its annual visit to Washington.   _____

8. Constructed of cedar, brick, and redwood, the new mountain cabins will endure many decades.   _____

9. A schoolbus driver must undergo special training and purchase a chauffeur's license in order to be hired by any board of education or private school.   _____

10. Although most states have laws and regulations that control interest rates, in many instances the laws are either confusing or contradictory. _____

Copyright © 1982 by Houghton Mifflin Company

Variety in Sentences 9.9

▶ *Make the following loose sentences into periodic ones.*

EXAMPLE

The liver is an irreplaceable organ of the body, for machines cannot duplicate
its various and highly complex functions.

Because machines cannot duplicate all of its various and highly complex bodily functions, one irreplaceable organ of the body is the liver.

1. The factory emptied quickly when the dinner bell rang.

   _____

   _____

2. I usually read a book in the evening after I have finished my work.

   _____

   _____

3. You must follow the directions carefully if you want to avoid making careless errors.

   _____

   _____

4. I hiked to Big Dry Creek and Little Dry Creek in east-central Montana.

   _____

   _____

5. The boy in the Darth Vader costume began to chew the gum he had
   received after he finished his Halloween candy.

   _____

   _____

6. South Dakota is nicknamed the Sunshine State, though many people prefer to call it the Coyote State.

   _____

7. Rodeo champions receive large sums of money each year, though not as much as other sports figures.

8. You will have to clean up the mess when you are finished.

9. Every stamp collector wants a 1928 Graf Zeppelin stamp because it is very rare.

10. The building was finished on the morning before the contract expired.

Copyright © 1982 by Houghton Mifflin Company

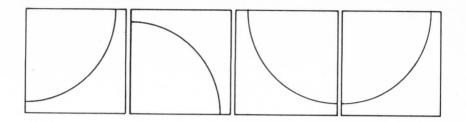

Punctuation

Uses of the comma
Although the comma has many functions, it is used, in general, to separate elements and to set off modifiers or parenthetical elements.

Between two independent clauses
Use the comma to separate independent clauses joined by a coordinating conjunction *(and, but, or, nor, for, so, yet)*.

The brisk winds raised only moderate waves, *but* the falling barometer indicated stormy weather was coming.

In a series
Use a comma between words, phrases, and clauses in a series.

We chose red, gold, and white for our color scheme. (words in a series)

The audience was seated, the overture had begun, and the curtain was about to open. (clauses in a series)

Between coordinate adjectives
Use a comma between **coordinate adjectives** not joined by *and*. Coordinate adjectives each modify the noun (or pronoun) independently.

The *gloomy, uninhabited* house was very isolated.

Cumulative adjectives do not modify independently. Do not use a comma between cumulative adjectives.

He discarded his *shabby old* clothes.

Note: to recognize coordinate adjectives, place the word *and* between them and determine whether they sound right.

The gloomy *and* uninhabited house was isolated. (sounds right)

He discarded his shabby *and* old clothes. (sounds wrong)

Another test is to reverse the adjectives. Normally, coordinate adjectives are easily reversible.

uninhabited, gloomy house (sounds right)

old shabby clothes (sounds wrong)

After long introductory clauses or phrases
Use a comma after a long introductory phrase or clause.

At the end of my first full day at work, I was ready for a good dinner. (phrase)

When my first full day at work ended, I was ready for a good dinner. (clause)

    Copyright © 1982 by Houghton Mifflin Company

Introductory verbal phrases usually are set off by a comma.

Working alone, she built a new room at the mountain retreat. (participial phrase)

To prepare for the race, the runner trained for weeks. (infinitive phrase)

After finishing dinner, we took a long walk. (prepositional phrase)

With nonrestrictive elements
Use commas to set off nonrestrictive appositives, phrases, and clauses that add description or information but are not essential to the meaning of the sentence.

Mary Evans, *the company comptroller,* was invited to a meeting in Washington. (nonrestrictive appositive phrase)

Mary Evans, *who is the company comptroller,* was invited to a meeting in Washington. (nonrestrictive adjective clause)

Note that a restrictive element is *never* set off by commas, since it is necessary for the meaning of the total sentence.

The music *that we most enjoy* is contemporary.

With parenthetical elements
Use commas with parenthetical elements.

We are prepared to continue the project, *we believe,* if there is enough public interest.

With conjunctive adverbs
Use a comma after a conjunctive adverb (*however, nevertheless, moreover, furthermore,* and so on) when it precedes an independent clause.

The profit margin was down; *however,* next year should be better.

With unusual word order
Use commas with sentence elements out of normal word order.

The cowboy, *haggard and thin,* slowly saddled his horse.

With degrees, titles, dates, places, addresses
Use commas with degrees and titles, as well as to separate elements in dates, places, and addresses.

Rosa Adams, M.D., joined the staff. (comma before and after *M.D.*)

On March 10, 1971, my daughter was born. (comma before and after year)

On Monday, December 19, the Christmas vacation begins.

In July 1969 we bought a new home. (optional commas)

The year 1945 marked the end of World War II. (no comma)

Sedona, Arizona, is at the entrance to Oak Creek Canyon. (Use a comma before and after the name of a state.)

My new address is 196 Warner Avenue, Westwood, California 73520. (no comma before zip code)

For contrast or emphasis

Use commas for contrast and emphasis as well as for short interrogative elements.

I want the new price list, not this one.

The dog stood still, not moving a muscle.

I was correct, wasn't I?

With mild interjections and *yes* or *no*

Use commas with mild interjections and with words like *yes* and *no*.

Well, I was almost right.

Yes, we agree to your offer.

With direct address

Use commas with words in direct address.

"Roberta, I need your help."

Use commas with expressions like *he said* or *she replied* when used with quoted matter.

"I cannot find my raincoat," *he complained.*

With absolute phrases

Set off an **absolute phrase** with a comma. An absolute phrase, which consists of a noun followed by a modifier, modifies an entire sentence.

The restaurant being closed, we decided to go home.

To prevent misreading or to mark an omission

Use commas to prevent misreading or to mark an omission.

Above, the wind howled through the trees.

The summer days were hot and dry; the night, warm and humid. (comma for omitted verb *was*)

   Copyright © 1982 by Houghton Mifflin Company

Unnecessary commas

Between subject and verb
Do not use a comma between subject and verb, between verb or verbal and complement, or between an adjective and the word it modifies.

NOT

The team with the best record, will go to the playoffs.

We saw, that the window had been left open.

The shining wrapping, paper got one's attention.

Between compound elements
Do not use a comma between compound elements, such as verbs, subjects, complements, and predicates.

NOT

We went to the local library, and perused *The New York Times.* (compound verb; comma unnecessary)

Between dependent clauses
Do not use a comma before a coordinating conjunction joining two dependent clauses.

NOT

We checked to see that the lights were off, and that all the doors were locked. (comma unnecessary)

In comparisons
Do not use a comma before *than* in a comparison or between compound conjunctions such as *as . . . as, so . . . so, so . . . that.*

NOT

The electrician found more wrong with the washing machine, than we had expected.

It was so hot, that the engine overheated.

After *like, such as*
Do not use a comma after *like* or *such as.*

NOT

Many famous paintings such as, the *Mona Lisa* and *View of Toledo* are almost priceless.

A comma is used before *such as* only when the phrase is nonrestrictive.

Do not use a comma directly before or after a period, a question mark, an exclamation point, or a dash.

NOT

"Were you late for work?", he asked.

With parentheses

A comma may follow a closing parenthesis but may not come before an opening parenthesis.

After reading *A Tale of Two Cities* (written by Charles Dickens), one understands the complexity of the French Revolution.

Other unnecessary commas

Do not use commas after coordinating conjunctions.

NOT

We did not like the accommodations at the hotel, but, we found nothing else available. (Retain comma before *but;* delete comma after *but*.)

A comma is not required after short adverbial modifiers.

After a rain the desert blooms with wildflowers. (no comma required after *rain*)

Do not use commas to set off restrictive clauses, phrases, or appositives.

NOT

The water level, *at the lake,* is low. (restrictive prepositional phrase)

Do not use a comma between adjectives that are cumulative and not coordinate. (See p. 148.)

FAULTY

The new, Persian rug was beautiful.

   Copyright © 1982 by Houghton Mifflin Company

NAME _____

DATE _____ SCORE _____

The Comma with Independent Clauses   10.1

▶ *In the following sentences, insert and encircle commas between independent clauses. In the blank at the right, enter the comma and the coordinating conjunction. If a sentence is correct, write C.*

EXAMPLE

The wheel of fortune was a significant symbol in many ancient cultures and it appears in the works of both Dante and Chaucer.   *,and*

1. Campers set up their tents and then they began to prepare dinner.   _____

2. The city's records are carefully kept up-to-date and are stored in a fireproof vault.   _____

3. At last someone has invented a glue that is almost permanent and that does not adhere to the skin.   _____

4. The Labrador retriever sat in the back of the pickup truck and it seemed to enjoy the wind blowing in its face.   _____

5. The attendants moved the animals from their small cages and relocated them in surroundings that approximated their natural habitats.   _____

6. The value of an entire coin collection mainly depends on the worth of a few rare pieces and on the condition of all the coins in a set.   _____

7. Hundreds of people crowded around the exhibit, and they appeared to enjoy the ones that provided live entertainment.   _____

8. The company's comptroller personally approved all vouchers for travel expenses and warned all employees against overspending.   _____

9. The diver realized the danger in attempting a new record

height in the brisk wind but he asked the judges for permission to raise the platform. ———

10. Many restaurants in New England are famous for their seafood and some also have fine views of the Atlantic Ocean and the fishing boats that sail along the coast. ———

Copyright © 1982 by Houghton Mifflin Company

The Comma with Independent Clauses   10.2

▶ *In the following sentences, insert and encircle commas between independent clauses. In the blank at the right, enter the comma and the coordinating conjunction. If a sentence is correct, write* C.

1. The costs of paper and postage continue to rise yet magazine sales remain brisk. _____

2. Vacationing in Hawaii is exciting but traveling closer to home is less expensive. _____

3. Many students seek part-time employment during their vacations so unemployment rates rise during the summer months. _____

4. Patience, persistence, and determination are necessary to train a dog but the most important requirement is consistency. _____

5. Many of the books in the library were very old and the librarian knew there was little money available to save them. _____

6. The docks were empty when the ship began to approach but suddenly they came alive with workers ready to unload the cargo. _____

7. Ub Iwerks was a famous animator and special-effects director at Disney Studios but few people have ever noticed his name on the screen. _____

8. Dr. Cagnilia kicked his golf ball out of the sand trap, but his playing partner caught him. _____

9. Infrared photographs of the earth's geography help scientists to determine the extent of droughts and they also are invaluable aids in the search for mineral deposits. _____

10. Fruits and vegetables usually are harvested before they are very ripe because most of them are canned commercially but a few are picked later and ultimately are sold as dried foods. ———

Copyright © 1982 by Houghton Mifflin Company

The Comma with Items in Series   10.3

▶ *Insert commas as necessary in items in series.*

EXAMPLE

Three novels by Kurt Vonnegut, Jr., are *Cat's Cradle, Slaughterhouse-Five,* and *Breakfast of Champions.*

1. Fuel oil natural gas and electricity are the most widely used sources of home energy.

2. American English continually drops old words adds new ones and develops new connotations for familiar expressions.

3. All the lights were on the stereo played loudly and the revelers continued to celebrate until morning.

4. Many recreational vehicles have complete kitchens that include compact refrigerators ranges and sinks.

5. The siren frightened the children, who ran inside climbed trees or hid in the shrubbery.

6. Many families purchase garden tractors for mowing hauling and cultivating.

7. "We've itemized deductions computed our refund and now must sign our tax returns," sighed the weary husband.

8. "During the Great Depression," my grandmother said, "many farmers refused government help shared food with neighbors and labored in one another's fields."

9. Birds eat harmful insects scatter seeds and spread pollen; thus they serve a variety of ecological functions.

10. "Since this inflation began, we have been in debt we are in debt and we will be in greater debt if we don't stop spending so much," moaned the anguished couple.

Copyright © 1982 by Houghton Mifflin Company

The Comma with Coordinate Adjectives 10.4

▶ *Insert commas as necessary between coordinate adjectives.*

EXAMPLE
The huge, gnarled oak was over a century old.

1. Colorful lightweight suits often are worn for formal occasions.

2. The bright cheerful greeting made me feel welcome.

3. Alfredo responded with quick intelligent answers when asked about his native Spain.

4. The model was a tall dark-haired strikingly attractive woman in her late twenties.

5. The carpenter worked long hard hours on the new addition.

6. The traffic study showed that many automobiles were using the new well-designed by-pass.

7. Many people now enjoy sturdy inexpensive trampolines in their yards.

8. The student of interior design must learn the modern energy-efficient ways of accent lighting.

9. A royal wedding requires months of careful detailed planning.

10. "Laughter, I believe, is the best least expensive medicine," said the speaker.

Copyright © 1982 by Houghton Mifflin Company

The Comma After Introductory Clauses or Phrases 10.5

▶ *Place commas as needed after introductory clauses or phrases. In the space at the right, place the comma and write the word before it. If no comma is necessary in any sentence, write* C.

EXAMPLE

Because the administration wanted to stimulate the economy, it recommended a tax rebate.

_____, it_____

1. When I came back from horseback riding I told my sister I wanted to buy a horse.   _____

2. Although Michael liked playing in the orchestra he did not like practicing.   _____

3. During the holidays the large crowds attend annual Christmas parades.   _____

4. Because the storm had torn down the power lines the family had to spend the night in a motel.   _____

5. Some experts say that the population explosion is the dominant problem of the twentieth century.   _____

6. How a frustrated candidate controls himself and his ardent followers in defeat may determine his chances for another political race in the future.   _____

7. Although I was a good football player my brother was better than I.   _____

8. When any newspaper prints what may be a libelous article it is usually quick to publish a retraction.   _____

9. Although citizens-band radios are not as powerful as short-wave sets they nevertheless furnish
   hours of enjoyment to many motorists.   _____

10. "Whatever we do this Saturday," Victor said, "I
    want to be home in time for the wrestling pro-
    gram on television."   _____

Copyright © 1982 by Houghton Mifflin Company

The Comma After Introductory Clauses or Phrases 10.6

▶ *Place commas as needed after introductory clauses or phrases. In the space provided at the right, place the comma and write the word before it. If no comma is necessary in any sentence, write* C.

1. After the demise of vaudeville many of its stars became radio and television entertainers. _____

2. Although we were separated by hundreds of miles, we remained friends and wrote often. _____

3. Even though the meeting was considered a success many in the group felt much of the work remained unfinished. _____

4. Freshly painted and renovated as a camper the used van sold as soon as it went on the market. _____

5. Stepping into her limousine the diplomat suddenly turned and waved to the crowd. _____

6. On the last day of our summer vacation we reluctantly cleaned up our cabin and began to pack the car. _____

7. Because doctors, parents, and students are requesting it physical hygiene is being taught in many public schools. _____

8. Although most of Mars' visible water now appears as polar ice and atmospheric vapor water may have flowed in rivers on the Martian surface thousands of years ago. _____

9. We found the exhibits at the museum interesting, although we thought some of them were in poor condition. _____

10. Until my ship actually sailed for the Far East, I never imagined that I would ever have the opportunity to see Japan. _____

Copyright © 1982 by Houghton Mifflin Company

The Comma with Nonrestrictive Elements   **10.7**

▶ *Correctly punctuate nonrestrictive elements in the following sentences. Write C to the right of any correctly punctuated sentence. Circle punctuation that you add.*

EXAMPLE

In Western culture the city of Babylon₍ᵧ₎much like Carthage₍ᵧ₎has
come to symbolize corruption and despair.   _____

1. The man talking to the bank manager is my father.   _____

2. Pier fishing which is especially popular in this area, shall
   remain unregulated.   _____

3. The ornate weather vanes that once topped most American homes are again becoming popular.   _____

4. The letter that I wrote today should be in Portland by
   Thursday.   _____

5. Dr. Pamela M. Smith who is the Vice President for Continuing Education delivered the commencement address.   _____

6. Many psychologists, some of whom spoke at a recent conference, believe that most three-year-olds can learn several languages.   _____

7. Blueberries which may be cultivated in large orchards
   make splendid jellies and jams.   _____

8. Governmental policy on price supports for commodities
   a subject of longstanding controversy will be revised to-
   tally during the next four years.   _____

9. Professional counseling in elementary school which is a
   relatively new field can make a dramatic difference in
   the scholastic performance of young children.   _____

10. Battery-powered fire alarms for homes should detect particles of combustion from three stages of a fire: the initial stage when invisible particles are produced by combustion without noticeable smoke or flame; the smoke stage when invisible particles of combustion become visible; and the flame stage when visible combustion is accompanied by rapid and destructive flames. ———

Copyright © 1982 by Houghton Mifflin Company

The Comma—All Uses   10.8

▶ *Correctly punctuate the following sentences. Circle punctuation that you add.*

EXAMPLE

Denver, Colorado, and Atlanta, Georgia, are two of the most rapidly growing cities in the United States.

1. On July 1 1981 we will begin a new training program for our older employees.

2. Alicia McMurray C.P.A. was employed by the firm of Feldman Parsons and Ames.

3. People seeking vocational advice may write to the Department of Labor Washington D.C. or they may call a regional office of their state employment service.

4. "In conclusion" said the long-winded dull speaker "I would like to thank all of you for coming—men women boys girls—all of you."

5. The international Morse code a form of the original Morse code used in international telegraphy is sometimes called the continental code.

6. Whenever we hear that snow has fallen in the nearby mountains we pack up the car and spend the weekend there.

7. The American Council of Learned Societies located at 345 East 46th Street New York New York 10017 sponsors many kinds of fellowships in various academic disciplines.

8. Hikers in the Appalachian Mountains need contour maps rather than road maps especially for the high ridges of the Pisgah National Forest.

9. "Although it is a relatively small city Bismarck North Dakota is the state capital and is twice as large as Pierre South Dakota which is also a state capital" stated the visiting lecturer in Geography 101.

10. Sandra O'Connor a jurist from Arizona is the first woman appointed to the United States Supreme Court.

Copyright © 1982 by Houghton Mifflin Company

The Comma—All Uses 10.9

▶ *Correctly punctuate the following sentences. Circle punctuation that you add.*
Write C in the blank at the right if the sentence is correct.

1. Many Americans are resisting the use of the metric system, even though it is used in science and throughout the world. _____

2. Any citizen of the United States may communicate with the President simply by addressing a letter to 1600 Pennsylvania Avenue Washington D.C. _____

3. Although pumice is quite porous and even appears to be spongy it is a form of volcanic rock used as an abrasive. _____

4. "The Book Exchange" the notice read "will be open on Monday December 19." _____

5. To settle legal disputes among themselves many nations turn to the International Court of Justice the main judicial body of the United Nations. _____

6. Some of the guests enjoyed the novelty of eating crab meat but most found it too salty. _____

7. The eager hardworking volunteers worked to complete the homecoming float. _____

8. Lifting the antique glass to the light to examine its color, examining the engraving and lightly tapping its sides the expert judged it to be quite valuable. _____

9. To a shaggy long-haired dog who can find little relief from the summer heat a cool bare concrete floor is a great blessing. _____

10. In the faculty's opinion students should be taught the seriousness of plagiarism. To steal money is unlawful; to steal someone's ideas unpardonable. ———

 Copyright © 1982 by Houghton Mifflin Company

Unnecessary Commas **10.10**

▶ *Circle all unnecessary commas in the following sentences.*

EXAMPLE
A citizen, who never votes, should not criticize elected officials.

1. The mountains near our home are noted for the beautiful, clear lakes, and the many, types of birds and plants.

2. The ferocious, black hornet is really a member of the wasp family, and, is, believe it or not, a very social insect.

3. The dingo, a wolf-like, wild, dog of Australia, is a natural enemy of sheep herds.

4. In *The Red Badge of Courage,* Stephen Crane brings to life, the psychological conflicts of young Henry Fleming, the hero.

5. An unusually large, black, bat quickly flew from room to room in the caverns, several hundred feet underground.

6. Of some botanical interest, is a plant called, rattlesnake root, which has tubers that supposedly cure rattlesnake bites—, at least many early settlers thought so.

7. The famous, Oregon Trail covered two thousand miles of frontier from Independence, Missouri, to Portland, Oregon, and was heavily traveled, during the westward migrations of the nineteenth century.

8. The written language of ancient Assyria and Babylonia, was characterized by cuneiform characters; that is, many of its letters were wedged-shaped, or, in other words, slim, triangular elements.

9. The so-called horse latitudes, which lie about thirty degrees, north and south, of the equator, are known for many calms, caused by high atmospheric pressure.

10. The phrase "horse latitudes," has two, possible derivations; the more likely one is that horses aboard ship may have died from starvation, because of the prolonged calms.

Copyright © 1982 by Houghton Mifflin Company

Unnecessary Commas 10.11

▶ *Circle all unnecessary commas in the following sentences.*

EXAMPLE

Edward and Nancy, graduated earlier than expected.

1. "A gentleman, sir," he quoted, "kneels only to pray, or propose. Furthermore, a gentleman removes his tie, only for sleeping.

2. When invited to an informal cookout, she appears, in fashionable, attire of fiery, red, and orange, silk; and her husband, always, wears a baggy, wrinkled, brown suit.

3. Of all the poems I have read recently, Thomas Hardy's lyric, "The Darkling Thrush," and Alfred, Lord Tennyson's, *In Memoriam,* seem the most pertinent to our times.

4. The shadow of the massive, ageless, oak fell upon the young, and carefree lovers, as they planned with infinite faith, for the future.

5. So great was the influence of Thomas Paine, on his own time, that John Adams suggested, that the era be called, "The Age of Paine."

6. One should never be ashamed, however, of being somewhat sentimental, for, a certain amount of sentimentality, can help keep a person warm and human.

7. By 1910, some demographers predicted, that the population of Western Europe would begin to decline, and that, by the end of the century, Eastern Europe would be more populous than Western Europe.

8. During the First World War and the Second World War, women replaced men in many factories and offices, but not until the latter war, did they form a branch of the armed services.

9. For France and Britain, the cause of the Seven Years' War was the desire for power over the growing, international economy, power

based on naval supremacy, and meaningful political control of colonies in the New World.

10. The physical conversion of heat, to mechanical energy, is presently accomplished by several kinds of engines,—the internal, combustion engine, the steam turbine, the gas turbine, and the awesome, rocket engine.

Copyright © 1982 by Houghton Mifflin Company

Semicolon, Colon, Dash, Parentheses, Brackets   11

The semicolon

Between two independent clauses

Use a semicolon between independent clauses not joined by *and, but, or, nor, for, so, yet.*

We hiked to the top of the mountain; we looked out over a valley covered with wildflowers.

Use a semicolon with a conjunctive adverb when it is followed by an independent clause.

We stayed until late afternoon; then we made our way back to camp.

Use a semicolon to separate independent clauses that are long and complex or that have internal punctuation.

Central City, located near Denver, was once a mining town; but now it is noted for its summer opera program.

Between items in a series

Use semicolons in a series between items that have internal punctuation.

In his closet Bill kept a photograph album, which was empty; several tennis shoes, all with holes in them; and the radiator cap from his first car, which he sold his first year in college.

Do not use a semicolon between elements that are not coordinate.

INCORRECT

After publishing *The Day of the Jackal* and several other popular novels; Frederick Forsyth wrote his most exciting book, *The Devil's Alternative.* (Use a comma, not a semicolon.)

The colon

Use the colon before quotations, statements, and series that are introduced formally.

The geologist began his speech with a disturbing statement: "This country is short of rare metals."

Use a colon to introduce a formal series.

Bring the following items: food for a week, warm clothes, bedding, and a canteen.

Between two independent clauses

Use a colon between two independent clauses when the second explains the first.

The team's record was excellent: we have not lost a game this season.

For special uses

Use the colon between hours and minutes.

4:35 P.M.

Unnecessary colon

Do not use a colon *after* a linking verb or a preposition.

INCORRECT

Our representatives are: Anne Crane and Andrew Miles.

He was accustomed to: hard work, good pay, and long weekends.

The dash

Use the dash to introduce summaries or to show interruption, parenthetical comment, or special emphasis.

For summary

Clothing, blankets, food, medicine—anything will help.

For interruption

"I want to say how sad—I mean happy—I am to be here," the speaker stumbled.

For parenthetical comments

This is important—I mean really important—so listen carefully.

For special emphasis

The key to the mystery could only be in one place—the attic.

Parentheses

Use parentheses to enclose loosely related comments or explanations or to enclose numbers used to indicate items in a series.

That year (1950) was the happiest time of my life.

Please do the following: (1) fill out the form, (2) include a check or money order, and (3) list any special mailing instructions.

Brackets

Use brackets to enclose *interpolations,* that is, the writer's explanations, within a passage that is being quoted.

The senator objected, "I cannot agree with your [Senator Miner's] reasoning." (brackets used to set off writer's interpolation)

Copyright © 1982 by Houghton Mifflin Company

The Semicolon   11.1

▶ *Insert semicolons where they are needed in the following sentences. If necessary, cross out other marks of punctuation. Circle semicolons that you add.*

EXAMPLE

Sociology may be generally defined as the study of the basic laws of all social
relations; social psychology, however, may be more narrowly described as the
study of the reciprocal influences of individuals and groups.

1. In 1900 the average life expectancy for an American was 47.3 years,
   in 1975 this average had increased to 72.4 years.

2. Some railroads use simulated locomotives to train engineers others
   depend on the traditional apprenticeship system.

3. An increase of dust particles in the earth's atmosphere may cause a
   general climatic cooling trend, they reflect sunlight and reduce solar heat.

4. Australia's Bicentennial gift to the United States was an endowed
   chair in Australian studies at Harvard University, another gift is a
   copy of Magna Charta from Great Britain.

5. Large banks may allow small, efficient data-processing firms to
   compute some of their paperwork, for example, payroll processing
   and stock transfers are often the work of contracted accounting
   firms.

6. Scientific prediction of earthquakes remains primitive and haphaz-
   ard, nevertheless, scientists can make general predictions after
   monitoring magnetic charges along major faults.

7. Automatic transmission and air conditioning account for higher au-
   tomotive fuel costs: for a luxury, eight-cylinder car the additional
   cost per ten thousand miles may reach $350, for a compact car, $150,
   and for a six-cylinder subcompact, $200.

8. Should the earth experience a slight rise in average temperature, polar ice would melt, consequently, ocean levels would rise, global wind patterns would change, rainfall levels would fluctuate, and agricultural production might be curtailed dramatically in presently fertile areas.

9. In the late nineteenth century, physicians believed that disease was caused almost exclusively by germs, now medical scientists know that diseases may have several causes—genetic aberrations, behavioral problems, such as smoking, drinking, or eating too much, and environmental causes, such as industrial pollution or social stress.

10. Chemicals made from hydrocarbons include ethyl alcohol, acetylene, used for welding, and ethylene glycol, which is a major ingredient of antifreeze.

Copyright © 1982 by Houghton Mifflin Company

The Semicolon 11.2

▶ *Insert semicolons where they are needed in the following sentences. If necessary, cross out other marks of punctuation. Circle semicolons that you add.*

EXAMPLE

The work was strenuous⨟in fact, the workers were exhausted.

1. The city manager proposed a graduated income tax, the city council preferred a citywide sales tax to increase revenues.

2. To the early Mormon settlers, the Colorado Plateau was unattractive, to later pioneers, it was a pastoral vista of tranquility and color.

3. Vinyl, which resembles leather, is a popular covering for contemporary-style sofas, cotton velvet, which resembles suede, is almost as popular.

4. Epoxy glue can join together almost any kind of material, except rubber and some plastics, indeed, the bond from the glue is often stronger than the original material.

5. Prospective pet owners should investigate thoroughly what kinds of animals best fit their lifestyles then the pets they choose may become pleasures rather than nuisances to them.

6. When purchasing an automobile battery, the consumer should compare various brands and sizes, standards of comparison may include a battery's cold-cranking power, reserve capacity, ampere-hour capacity, and total number of plates.

7. A good set of tools should include a socket wrench, with various sockets and adapters, screwdrivers, conventional and Phillips' head, a hacksaw, and a hammer.

8. Rapid movement in fleeing a predator is, for many insects, a pri-

mary means of surviving, escaping detection through protective coloration is also a basic survival technique.

9. A *biome* is a large geographical area with similar topographical and climatic characteristics, the eastern United States, for instance, has a deciduous forest biome, the plains states have a grassland biome, the southwestern states, a desert biome, and Alaska has a tundra biome.

10. To fight increased electrical costs, a homeowner might install an attic fan, an attic ventilator, which is essentially an attic fan mounted on a gable, or a roof ventilator, which mounts on a roof or a gable and which turns by electrical power or simply by the force of the wind.

   Copyright © 1982 by Houghton Mifflin Company

Colons and Dashes   11.3

▶ *Correctly punctuate the following sentences. Circle punctuation that you add.*
Write C to the left of any sentence that is correct.

EXAMPLE
All of New England(—)Connecticut, Maine, Massachusetts, New Hampshire, Rhode Island, and Vermont(—)is likely to suffer serious fuel shortages during bad winters.

1. The quarterback's play a tight-end screen pass surprised both the defense and the fans.

2. Many theaters find that an 815 curtain time means fewer latecomers than one at 800.

3. The cotton gin invented by a man from Massachusetts on a visit to Georgia helped to shape the economic destinies of both North and South.

4. A good bird watcher makes identifications using the following characteristics voice, color, size, type of bill, markings, and range.

5. There is one quality that endears two-year-olds to those around them their desire to imitate adults.

6. Ragweed, mesquite, pine all produce common allergies.

7. The most common means of evaluation the intelligence test is no longer considered sufficient as the sole criterion for placement in special classes.

8. The school board president made a startling announcement "Fellow citizens, you may keep your children home tomorrow. We must allow a complete day for general repairs."

9. Most biblical scholars agree that the twentieth century has witnessed one of the most significant archeological discoveries of all time namely, the Dead Sea Scrolls.

10. The weather reporter announced, "There will be snow excuse me that should be rain tonight."

Copyright © 1982 by Houghton Mifflin Company

Parentheses and Brackets 11.4

▶ *Insert parentheses and brackets where they are needed in the following sentences. Circle parentheses and brackets that you add.*

EXAMPLE

The donkey (descended from *Equus asinus*) is a domesticated wild ass.

1. The administration of Franklin D. Roosevelt 1932–1945 was the longest of any President.

2. Saint Valentine's Day February 14 is observed in honor of a Christian martyr.

3. Boise which rhymes with "noisy" is the capital of Idaho; it was built on the Oregon Trail.

4. The agronomist considered soybeans as the crop of the future because 1 they have few natural enemies; 2 they are high in protein; and 3 they require relatively little expensive fertilizer.

5. Seventeen thousand new Flashback cars the model had just been introduced had to be recalled because of faulty brakes.

6. The expert on etiquette she had written four books on the subject concluded: "Good manners reveal it good breeding; therefore, one should take it seriously."

7. Many physicians believe that most people would enjoy good health if they would a eat modestly, b exercise regularly, and c maintain an optimistic attitude.

8. The shrimpboat captain told his crew: "they he meant the shrimp are making a comeback."

9. As Professor Nichols explains, "It the study of cinema is still in its infancy."

10. Benjamin Franklin 1709–1790 said: "No morning sun lasts a whole day."

Quotation Marks and End Punctuation   12

Quotation marks
Use quotation marks to enclose the exact words of a speaker or writer.

"I'm tired," he said. (declarative statement and object of verb *said*)

"Come here," she demanded. (command)

"Who's ready to leave?" Mary asked. (question)

"Quick!" he shouted. (exclamation)

Periods and *commas* always are placed inside quotation marks. *Semicolons* and *colons* always are placed outside quotation marks. *Question marks* and *exclamation points* are placed inside quotation marks when they refer to the quotation itself. They are placed outside the quotation marks when they refer to the entire sentence.

Who said, "We need a new car"? (Quotation is a statement.)

Use quotation marks to enclose dialogue. Do not use quotation marks with indirect quotation.

Alexander Pope once wrote, "A little learning is a dangerous thing." (direct quotation)

Alexander Pope said that a little learning can be dangerous. (indirect quotation)

In dialogue a new paragraph marks each change of speaker.

"Do you have change for a dollar?" the customer asked, after searching in his pocket for change.
"I think so," replied the cashier.

Quotation within a quotation
Use single quotation marks to enclose a quotation within a quotation.

John complained, "I don't understand your comment, 'Be clear first, then clever.' "

Titles
Use quotation marks to enclose the titles of essays, articles, short stories, chapters, television programs, and short musical compositions.

We enjoy reading William Safire's column, "On Language," in the Sunday newspaper. (article in newspaper)

Many people do not know whether to like or to hate the CBS program "60 Minutes." (television program)

The band began to play Sousa's "Stars and Stripes Forever." (musical composition)

    Copyright © 1982 by Houghton Mifflin Company

Unnecessary quotations

Do not use quotation marks to emphasize or change the usual meanings of words or to point out the use of slang or attempts at humor.

NOT

We had a "great" time at the party. (emphasis)

That movie was really "bad." (change of meaning)

I guess we "goofed." (slang)

His lemonades are so bad that they always turn out to be "lemons." (attempted humor)

End punctuation

Use a **period** after sentences that make statements and after sentences that express command which is not exclamatory.

The humidity made us uncomfortable. (statement)

Meet us after the concert. (mild command)

Use a **question mark** after a direct question.

What time is it?

Use an **exclamation point** after a word, a phrase, or a sentence to indicate strong feeling.

Ouch! That hurt!

Stop that man!

Remember to use a period after mild exclamations.

That is the craziest idea I ever heard.

Copyright © 1982 by Houghton Mifflin Company

NAME _____

DATE _____ SCORE _____

Quotation Marks and End Punctuation   12.1

▶ *Correctly punctuate the following sentences. Circle any* incorrect *punctuation and indicate what punctuation should be used. Indicate a new paragraph with the sign* ¶.

EXAMPLE

"What kind of trees are those⟨,⟩" asked the tourist. "Redwoods," replied the ranger.

1. My ring is gone cried the frantic woman.

2. "Well!" the sergeant said, you don't have my permission."

3. Keep your bike in top condition for safe riding said the instruction booklet.

4. What sort of experience leads a young person to choose the life of a surgeon inquired the patient.

5. The social scientist summarized as follows: Because young people generally have values in opposition to those of adult society, youth can be classified as a genuine subculture.

6. An increase in radon in well water said the science reporter may become a means for geologists to predict earthquakes.

7. So many foreign visitors were anticipated by Greek officials that they made arrangements for several ships to provide accommodations for tourists without hotel reservations explained the travel agent.

8. Stop You've tried my patience to the limit

9. The press corps asked exactly what the role of the President's science adviser would be?

10. Did you know that some of the officers in the American Revolution came to this country from Poland specifically to help us win the war

asked the history instructor. Our town, Pulaski, Tennessee, is named for one of them a student answered. Correct that was Count Pulaski responded the teacher.

Copyright © 1982 by Houghton Mifflin Company

Quotation Marks and End Punctuation   12.2

▶ *Correctly punctuate the following sentences. Circle any incorrect punctuation. Indicate a new paragraph with the sign ¶.*

EXAMPLE
The boy's cry, **"**Help**!** I'm hurt,**"** went unheard.

1. The article discussed why boys and girls differ in behavior even before puberty?

2. To freeze peaches droned the television chef use citric acid to prevent the fruit from turning brown.

3. Although "considered strange" by his friends, Raymond was actually only very shy.

4. "Why do I have to go to the dentist," the child asked?

5. "Who said, "The only place he'd be the life of the party is in a mortuary?"

6. Quick the driver screamed to the passerby the light will change shortly.

7. When my daughter completes her B. S. continued the proud father she expects to begin work toward her M. S. and eventually to earn her Ph. D.

8. When the diner looked at the burned steak, he complained to the waiter, "I said well-done, not cremated". You said very well-done, sir replied the waiter.

9. The first entry on the syllabus for the survey of American literature began as follows: Emerson's essay, The American Scholar; Mark Twain's story, The Man That Corrupted Hadleyburg; and Frost's poem, After Apple-Picking.

10. The reporter asked the old man: What advice do you have for today's young people? Absolutely nothing the old man responded to the hackneyed question.

Copyright © 1982 by Houghton Mifflin Company

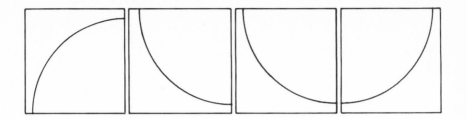

Mechanics

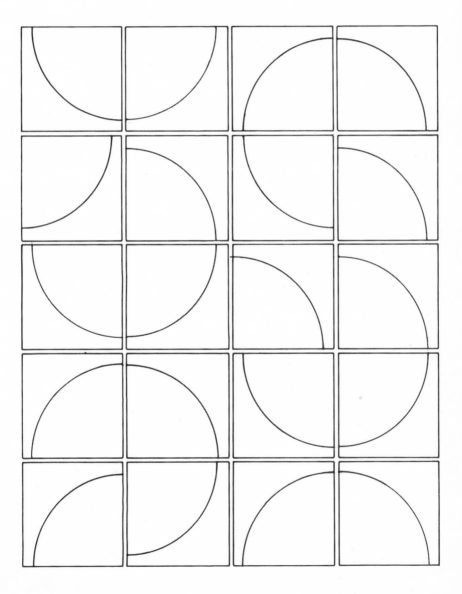

Dictionaries contain information that is necessary for precise writing. The following entry from the *American Heritage Dictionary* for the word *bureaucrat* indicates the kinds of information that are found in an entry. The numbers in brackets have been added.

bureaucrat [1] byŏŏr'ə-krăt) [2] *n.* [3] 1. An official of a bureaucracy. 2. Any official who insists on rigid adherence to rules, forms, and routines. [4]—bureaucratic *adj.* bureaucratically *adv.*

[5] *Usage:* In American usage *bureaucrat* is almost invariably derogatory, unless the context establishes otherwise.

After the word is the following information: (1) the pronunciation and syllabication of the word, (2) the part of speech, (3) the definitions of the word, (4) the ways the word is spelled for other parts of speech, and (5) the way the word is used.

Dictionaries also include the following:

1. Principal parts of regular and irregular verbs, degrees of adjectives and adverbs, and irregular forms of nouns
2. Comparative and superlative degrees of adjectives and adverbs
3. Plurals of nouns
4. Archaic forms of inflected verbs (*doest* for the second-person present tense of *do*)
5. Labels for the technical or limited use of words (*chemistry* or *sports,* for example)
6. Other labels indicating restricted usage (*nonstandard, slang, poetic, foreign languages*)
7. Cross-references to other words and spelling variations
8. Etymologies
9. Synonyms
10. Standard abbreviations
11. Miscellaneous information including references to famous people, to geographic areas, and to important historical movements and periods.

   Copyright © 1982 by Houghton Mifflin Company

The Dictionary: Etymologies   13.1

▶ *Using the dictionary find the original meaning of each of the following words.*

EXAMPLE
beret ___*cap, hooded cape*_____

1. snack _____

2. bonfire _____

3. left _____

4. sinister _____

5. gasket _____

6. insult _____

7. thug _____

8. oaf _____

9. mortmain _____

10. nag _____

11. horrible _____

12. pagan _____

13. giddy _____

14. summon _____

15. snob _____

16. mordant _____

17. sneak _____

18. umbrella _____

19. dwell _____

20. mercy _____

Copyright © 1982 by Houghton Mifflin Company

The Dictionary: Pronunciation and Parts of Speech   13.2

▶ *Using the dictionary write out the phonetic spelling and list the parts of speech for each of the following words.*

EXAMPLE
brass *brăs, bräs*   *noun*

	PHONETIC SPELLING	PARTS OF SPEECH
1. game		
2. equal		
3. invite		
4. romance		
5. material		
6. enough		
7. ensemble		
8. bully		
9. base		
10. gaze		
11. ornament		
12. sheer		
13. venture		
14. many		
15. ascendant		
16. head		
17. tertiary		
18. weld		
19. velvet		
20. remark		

Italicize (underline) titles of independent publications (books, magazines, newspapers) and, occasionally, words to be emphasized.

Underline titles of books (except the Bible and its divisions), periodicals, newspapers, motion pictures, musical compositions (operas and symphonies, for example), works of art, plays, and other works published separately.

Titles

Books
The World Almanac

Periodicals
Psychology Today

Newspapers
Washington Post or the Washington Post

Motion pictures
Star Wars

Musical compositions, paintings, and sculpture
Handel's Messiah

Rodin's The Thinker

Plays
The Tempest

Names of ships and trains
Underline the names of ships and trains.

the U.S.S. Nimitz

the Zephyr

Foreign words
Underline foreign words used in an English context if they have not become a part of our language. Check the dictionary before underlining foreign words.

The nachalstvo, the privileged class of Russian communist party members, are afforded the same luxuries available to the wealthy in any other country.

 Copyright © 1982 by Houghton Mifflin Company

Words being named

Underline words, letters, and figures being named.

The word credenza, which now refers to a table, once was associated with poison.

Your m's look like n's.

For occasional emphasis

Although underlining for emphasis is permissible on occasion, avoid excessive underlining because it often reveals a writer's weak vocabulary.

NOT

That's not just a big dinner. That's a big dinner.

IMPROVED

That's not just a big dinner. That's a feast.

Copyright © 1982 by Houghton Mifflin Company

Italics   **14.1**

▶ *Underline words that should be italicized in the following sentences.*

EXAMPLE
<u>Sanford</u> <u>and</u> <u>Son</u> continues as a favorite rerun.

1. The Old Man and the Sea is perhaps Hemingway's most popular novel.

2. Lorry is a British word for truck.

3. People learning to pronounce English as a foreign language often find l's, g's, and k's to be troublesome.

4. Virgil's Aeneid is the most famous long epic poem in Roman literature.

5. Millions of tourists see Charles Lindbergh's aircraft, the Spirit of St. Louis, at the Smithsonian Institution.

6. John Wayne's satiric performance in True Grit won him many accolades.

7. The United States Navy plans to recommission the U.S.S. New Jersey, a World War II battleship.

8. All in the Family, now replaced by Archie Bunker's Place, was one of the most popular shows in the history of modern television.

9. Kurt Vonnegut, Jr.'s, novel God Bless You, Mr. Rosewater, or Pearl's Before the Swine, was first published in 1965.

10. The decision was a fait accompli before any discussion concerning its implications.

Copyright © 1982 by Houghton Mifflin Company

Italics **14.2**

▶ *Underline for italics in the following sentences.*

EXAMPLE
<u>Audubon: A Vision</u> is a long poem by Robert Penn Warren.

1. The United States, not the Queen Elizabeth II, was the largest ocean liner ever built.

2. Roger Tory Peterson's A Field Guide to the Birds has been called the authorative book for bird watchers.

3. Good Housekeeping and Better Homes and Gardens are magazines for the home.

4. The word urbane has been used to describe magazines such as National Geographic and Discover.

5. The Tonight Show is the longest-running talk show in the history of television.

6. A roman à clef is a novel like Thomas Wolfe's Look Homeward, Angel, which presents real people and events under fictional guises.

7. Soap operas like As the World Turns and Ryan's Hope attract large audiences.

8. Vivaldi's The Four Seasons is a masterpiece of baroque music.

9. The Empire Strikes Back is a sequel to Star Wars.

10. The Washington Post is the only newspaper published in Washington, D.C.

Spell correctly. Use the dictionary when you are uncertain of the spelling.

Be particularly careful of words that are not spelled as they sound (*though* and *debt*), words that sound the same (*sew* and *so*), words with the "uh" sound, which gives no clue to their spelling (*terrible* and *persistent*).

Do not misspell words by omitting a syllable that is occasionally not pronounced (*accidently* for *accidentally*), by adding syllables (*mischievious* for *mischievous*), or by changing syllables (*preform* for *perform*).

Guides for spelling

For *ie* and *ei*
Use *i* before *e (believe)* except after *c (receive)* or when these letters are sounded as *a (neighbor)*. There are a few exceptions *(either, neither, leisure, seize, weird, height)*.

Final *e*
Drop the final *e* when adding a **suffix** if the suffix begins with a vowel *(dine* to *dining)*. Keep the *e* if the suffix begins with a consonant *(leave* to *leaving)*. There are some exceptions (for example, *notice* becomes *noticeable,* and *awe* becomes *awful.*)

For changing *y* to *i*
Change the *y* to *i* when the *y* is preceded by a consonant, but not when the *y* is preceded by a vowel or when *-ing* is added *(story* become *stories, delay* becomes *delays,* and *fly* becomes *flying)*.

Suffixes
If the suffix begins with a consonant, do not double the final consonant of a word *(quick* becomes *quickly)*. If the suffix begins with a vowel, double the last consonant of one-syllable words *(bat* becomes *batting)* and of words of more than one syllable if the accent is on the last syllable *(occúr* becomes *occurrence)*. Do not double the final consonant if that consonant is preceded by two vowels *(repair* becomes *repairing)*, or if the word ends with two or more consonants *(drink* becomes *drinking)*, or if the last syllable of the word is not pronounced after the suffix is added *(prefér* becomes *préference)*.

Plurals
Add *-s* for plurals of most nouns *(sound* becomes *sounds)* and for nouns ending in *o* when it is preceded by a vowel *(portfolio* becomes *portfolios)*. Add *-es* when the plural has another syllable that is pronounced *(speech*

Copyright © 1982 by Houghton Mifflin Company

becomes *speeches*) and in most cases when the noun ends in *o* preceded by a consonant (*tomato* becomes *tomatoes*). See a dictionary for the exceptions.

The plurals of proper names are generally formed by adding *-s* or *-es (Taylor, Taylors; Jones, Joneses)*.

Hyphenation and syllabication

Use a hyphen in certain compound words and in words divided at the end of a line.

It is best to consult a dictionary to determine whether a compound word is hyphenated or is written as one or two words. Hyphenate a compound of two or more words used as a single modifier before a noun.

HYPHEN	NO HYPHEN
He is a *well-known* millionaire.	The millionaire is *well known*.

Hyphenate spelled-out compound numbers from *twenty-one* through *ninety-nine*.

When hyphenating a word at the end of a line, do not divide one-syllable words, do not put a one-letter syllable on a separate line (*a-long*, for example) and avoid carrying over a two-letter suffix to another line (*pock-et*). Divide words according to the syllabication in the dictionary.

Copyright © 1982 by Houghton Mifflin Company

Spelling: Suffixes   15.1

▶ *In the blank spaces provided, write the correct spellings of the following words.*

EXAMPLE
cite / ing   *citing* _____

1. believe / able _____

2. occupy / ed _____

3. submit / ing _____

4. moral / ist _____

5. undesire / able _____

6. forbid / en _____

7. write / ing _____

8. symptom / atic _____

9. eat / able _____

10. real / istic _____

11. full / ness _____

12. like / able _____

13. subdue / ing _____

14. interchange / able _____

15. mass / ive _____

16. beauty / eous _____

17. commit / ing _____

18. reverse / ible _____

19. begin / ing _____

20. occur / ing _____

21. fry / ed _____

22. fry / ing _____

23. plural / istic _____

24. recur / ed _____

25. cancel / ed _____

 Copyright © 1982 by Houghton Mifflin Company

Spelling: Suffixes   15.2

▶ *In the blank spaces provided, write the correct spellings of the following words.*

EXAMPLE
stop / ing   _stopping_ _____

1. deserve / ing _____

2. mountain / ous _____

3. forbid / ing _____

4. forebode / ing _____

5. defer / ed _____

6. invalid / ate _____

7. true / ly _____

8. lone / liness _____

9. conceive / able _____

10. envy / able _____

11. net / ing _____

12. direct / ory _____

13. endure / ed _____

14. prescribe / ing _____

15. admit / ance _____

16. marvel / ous _____

17. travel / ed _____

18. adequate / ly _____

19. courage / ous _____

20. explore / ation _____

21. judge / ment _____

22. achieve / ment _____

23. pretty / ly _____

24. guarantee / ing _____

25. propose / al _____

Copyright © 1982 by Houghton Mifflin Company

Spelling: *ie* and *ei*   **15.3**

▶ *Fill in the blanks in the following words with* ie *or* ei.

EXAMPLE
defic___*ie*___nt

1. p_____rce

2. v_____n

3. f_____ry

4. rec_____ve

5. p_____ce

6. p_____r

7. financ_____r

8. s_____ve

9. dec_____t

10. _____ther

11. ser_____s

12. rel_____ve

13. v_____w

14. fr_____nd

15. n_____ce

16. for_____gn

17. f_____gn

18. conc_____ve

19. s_____ge

20. n_____ther

21. sc_____nce

22. rec_____pt

23. dec_____ve

24. h_____ght

25. s_____ze

  Copyright © 1982 by Houghton Mifflin Company

Spelling: *ie* and *ei*   **15.4**

▶ *Fill in the blanks in the following words with* ie *or* ei.

EXAMPLE
prem *ie* r

1. forf_____t

2. f_____ld

3. retr_____ve

4. consc_____nce

5. shr_____k

6. y_____ld

7. ach_____ve

8. d_____gn

9. fr_____ght

10. h_____r

11. conc_____t

12. consc_____ntious

13. n_____ghbor

14. r_____gn

15. sl_____gh

16. omnisc_____nt

17. n_____gh

18. bel_____ve

19. perc_____ve

20. w_____ght

21. l_____sure

22. c_____ling

23. spec_____s

24. sh_____ld

25. w_____rd

    Copyright © 1982 by Houghton Mifflin Company

Spelling: Plurals   15.5

▶ *Form the plural for each of the following nouns. If there is more than one plural form, give all of them. Consult your dictionary when in doubt.*

EXAMPLE
bush ___*bushes*___

1. wolf _____

2. villain _____

3. memorandum_____

4. spectrum _____

5. desk _____

6. cargo _____

7. gypsy _____

8. thief _____

9. antenna _____

10. oasis _____

11. antithesis _____

12. bookshelf _____

13. hero _____

14. committee _____

15. trauma _____

16. village _____

17. essay _____

18. cemetery _____

19. embargo_____

20. locust_____

21. halo _____

22. alumnus_____

23. manifesto _____

24. medium _____

25. criterion_____

Copyright © 1982 by Houghton Mifflin Company

Hyphenation   15.6

▶ *Write the correct spelling of the following compounds in the blanks at the right. If a spelling is correct, write C in the blank. Consult a recent dictionary.*

EXAMPLE
hat-less *hatless*
reenter *re-enter*

1. fiftytwo _____

2. get together _____

3. old fashioned _____

4. air conditioning _____

5. first rate _____

6. de escalate _____

7. one-hundred _____

8. trans continental _____

9. nation wide _____

10. laissez faire _____

11. baby sitter _____

12. one-twelfth _____

13. half truth _____

14. per centage _____

15. per cent _____

16. non fiction _____

17. thing in itself _____

18. hub bub _____

19. semi solid _____

20. great grandmother _____

21. pro American _____

22. all-purpose _____

23. re-write _____

24. excouncilman _____

25. sub-terranean _____

 Copyright © 1982 by Houghton Mifflin Company

Hyphenation and Syllabication   15.7

▶ *Circle errors in hyphenation or syllabication and correct them. Add hyphens where necessary.*

EXAMPLE

Two-tone⌒automobile exteriors remain very popular.

1. House-hold ammonia is a good detergent.

2. Some colleges require comprehensive-admissions tests.

3. John is a good hearted man with many well known qualities.

4. Inside the drug-store the pharmacist carefully filled the prescription.

5. Portuguese-men-of-war, which may inflict painful stings, often are blown in-land by tropical storms.

6. Physicians warn that quack remedies for arthritis—apple-cider, vinegar, a dry-climate, or a copper-bracelet—have no medical value.

7. Bills de-signed to ex-pand the active work force have been introduced in the House-of-Representatives.

8. Some political theorists believe that the Attorney-General should be independent of the White-House, and a congressional subcommittee is studying this suggestion.

9. The Department of Public Safety tries to discourage hitch hikers because many of them are victimized by so called Good Samaritan drivers.

10. An increase of white collar jobs, a decrease of blue collar jobs, and an increase in the number of working wives will mean that 30 per cent of all American families will earn $25,000 or more by 1985.

Apostrophes, Capitals, and Numbers   16

Apostrophes
Use the apostrophe for the possessive case of many nouns, contractions, omissions, and some plurals.

Use *'s* for the possessive of nouns not ending in *s*.

SINGULAR

child's, worker's

PLURAL

people's, women's

Use *'s* or *'* without the *s* for possessive of singular nouns ending in *s*. Do not add the *s* when a singular noun ending in *s* is followed by a word that begins with *s*.

Dennis's, or Dennis' *but not* Dennis's stories

Use *'* without the *s* to form the possessive of plural nouns ending in *s*.

the Howards' vacation, the actresses' dressing room

Use *'s* to form the possessive of indefinite pronouns.

anyone's, everybody's, neither's

Use *'s* with only the last noun when indicating joint possession in a pair or series.

Elizabeth and Bob's car was new. (They own the car together.)

Elizabeth's and Bob's cars were new. (They each own a car.)

Use *'* to show omissions or to form contractions.

the '80s, won't, it's (it is)

Use *'s* to form the plural of numerals, letters, and words being named.

five *9*'s, three *b*'s

Capital letters
Use a capital letter to begin a sentence and to designate a proper noun.

Capitalize the first word in a sentence, the letter *I*, and the interjection *O*.

What, O what, have I done?

Capitalize the first, last, and important words in titles, including the second part of hyphenated words.

Great Expectations

The Man with the Golden Horn

Slaughterhouse-Five

   Copyright © 1982 by Houghton Mifflin Company

Capitalize first words in quotations and words capitalized by the author.

"We could call this the Age of Indifference," the author wrote.

Capitalize titles preceding names.

Admiral Halsey

Capitalize titles of the leader of a nation even when the name of the person is not given. Capitalize titles that substitute for specific names.

The Prime Minister is in conference.

General Ames has been in Europe. The General has been inspecting NATO units.

A title not followed by a name is usually not capitalized.

The chairman counted the votes.

Titles which are common nouns that name an office are not capitalized.

A private has a hard life.

Capitalize degrees and titles after names.

Alice Trevor, Management Consultant

Denise Lattimore, M.D.

Capitalize words of family relationships used as names when not preceded by a possessive pronoun.

I know Dad will want to see the game.

Capitalize proper nouns and their derivatives.

Paris, Parisian; the Southwest; Democrats, the Democratic Party; the Missouri River; Middle Atlantic States

Capitalize movements, periods, and events in history.

the Victorian Period, the Spanish-American War

Capitalize movements, periods, and events in history.

the Victorian Period, the Spanish-American War

Capitalize words referring to the Deity, to religious denominations, and to religious literature. Pronouns referring to the Deity are usually capitalized.

God, Methodism, the Bible

We know He is our God.

Capitalize the titles of specific courses and the names of languages.

English 101, Mathematics 235

An English course *but not* a Math course (because not specific)

Abbreviations

Avoid most abbreviations in writing. Spell out the names of days, months, units of measurement, and (except in addresses) states and countries.

Monday (*not* Mon.); February (*not* Feb.); ounce (*not* oz.); Fort Worth, Texas (*not* Tex.)

Abbreviations are acceptable before names (Mr., Dr.), after names (Sr., D.D.S.), and with dates and time (B.C., A.D., and A.M., P.M.).

Numbers

Spell out numbers that can be written in one or two words.

forty-five, one hundred

Use figures for other numbers.

12367, $978.34, 3⅓

Never begin sentences with numbers. Rephrase the sentence or spell the numbers out.

NOT
50 men started work.

BUT
Fifty men started work.

OR
There were 50 men who started work.

Use numerals for figures in a series.

We bought 10 pounds of potatoes, 2 quarts of milk, and 2 dozen eggs.

Use figures for dates, street numbers, page references, percentages, and hours of the day used with A.M. or P.M.

USE FIGURES	SPELL OUT
March 7, 1981	the seventh of March
4511 Mary Ellen Avenue	Tenth Street
See page 10.	The book has twenty pages.
He paid 10 percent interest.	
The meeting starts at 10 P.M.	The meeting starts at ten o'clock.

Copyright © 1982 by Houghton Mifflin Company

The Apostrophe   16.1

▶ *Give the singular possessive and the plural possessive of the following nouns.*

EXAMPLE
campaign   *campaign's*   *campaigns'*

　　　　　　　　　SINGULAR POSSESSIVE　　　PLURAL POSSESSIVE

 1. chief   _____   _____

 2. woman   _____   _____

 3. child   _____   _____

 4. institution   _____   _____

 5. Jones (last

    name)   _____   _____

 6. marksman   _____   _____

 7. genius   _____   _____

 8. Perez (last

    name)   _____   _____

 9. druggist   _____   _____

10. dictionary   _____   _____

11. heroine   _____   _____

12. cemetery   _____   _____

13. poet   _____   _____

14. girl   _____   _____

15. fox   _____   _____

16. church   _____   _____

17. Mathis (last

    name)   _____   _____

18. attorney   _____   _____

19. mother-in-law   _____   _____

20. workman   _____   _____

21. specimen   _____   _____

22. Pakistani   _____   _____

23. Westerner   _____   _____

24. library   _____   _____

25. judge   _____   _____

Copyright © 1982 by Houghton Mifflin Company

The Apostrophe   16.2

▶ *Add apostrophes where necessary and circle incorrect apostrophes. Change spellings where appropriate.*

EXAMPLE
Almost everyone's imagination was electrified by the space flights of the '60s.

1. The Alvarezes new home was constructed on the top of a hill overlooking the city.

2. Its almost impossible for a new administrations policies to be effective immediately.

3. The outcome of the Metropolitan Operas regional auditions is anybodys guess.

4. Charles attitude toward his fellow workers changed when he knew them better and began to spend his evening's with them.

5. The Waitresses Guild decided to hold it's 78 convention in Chicago because of the citys' good accommodations.

6. Most of the attorneys day—from eight oclock until two oclock—is spent in hearings, committee meetings, and court sessions.

7. The groom followed his future father-in-laws advice and carefully hid his car before the wedding days festivities.

8. The calculator sputtered and erroneously registered eight 7s across the screen, and these were immediately followed by a series of Es.

9. The children said the toys were their's, not the neighbors children's.

10. The quarterbacks and the wide-receivers intuitions about the defenses plays made them an extraordinarily effective offensive combination.

Copyright © 1982 by Houghton Mifflin Company

Capitals 16.3

▶ *Correct the errors in capitalization.*

EXAMPLE
The most populous state is *C*alifornia.

1. Situation Comedies are often popular on Television.

2. *Gone with the wind,* perhaps the most famous movie of all times, has now been adapted for the stage.

3. William Faulkner said that his short Novel *As I lay dying* was a *tour de force.*

4. Many critics believe that Educational Television has matured because of its excellent production of Children's Programs.

5. The climax of Shakespeare's *King Richard III* comes when king Richard says, "a horse! a horse! my kingdom for a horse!"

6. The english word *Young* comes from the swedish word for heather, *ljung;* the english obviously changed *lj* into *y.*

7. Summer Stock Companies often make up in *esprit de corps* what they lack in theatrical sophistication and experience.

8. Winston Churchill, prime minister of great Britain during the second world war, was the unlikely author of a book on Art called *Painting for Pleasure.*

9. Eric Arthur Blair, known to the Public as George Orwell, was a British Essayist who satirized modern politicians for their use of such phrases as *render inoperative, militate against, make contact with, be subjected to,* and *make itself felt.*

10. The septuagint, one of the earliest texts of the bible, is the oldest Greek version of the old testament; Legend says that it was translated by seventy jewish scholars at the request of Ptolemy II of Egypt.

Copyright © 1982 by Houghton Mifflin Company

Abbreviations and Numbers   16.4

▶ *Correct unacceptable usage of abbreviations and numbers. Write corrections above the line.*

EXAMPLE   *Twenty-six*
2̶6̶ people arrived after 6 P.M., the hotel's deadline for holding reservations.

1. Most newscasts begin at 6 o'clock in the P.M. to attract 1000's of people who are home for dinner at this time.

2. Ernest Hemingway won the Nobel Prize for Lit. in nineteen hundred fifty-four.

3. Richard Smith, M.D., opened his practice in Sioux City, Ia., on Oct. twentieth, nineteen hundred eighty.

4. The Metro. Transit Authority purchased 22 new buses for two million, four hundred, forty thousand dollars.

5. Occupancy rates of hotels in some resort areas climbed as high as 90% during the Bicentennial celebration.

6. One lineman weighed two hundred fifty lbs.; another, two hundred forty lbs.; the third, two hundred sixty lbs.; and the last, two hundred eighty lbs.—all for an average weight of 257 pt. 5 lbs.

7. *The New York Times* sent its best reporters to Wash., D.C., to cover the White House, Sen., and House of Rep.

8. Economists agree that countries with fifty percent inflation are in deep financial trouble.

9. On the twenty-fourth of Dec. ea. year community choirs across the
   U.S. go caroling.

10. Rev. Smith, Sen. Alfonso, and Capt. Briggs of the A.F. were present
    for the commissioning of the new Lts.

Copyright © 1982 by Houghton Mifflin Company

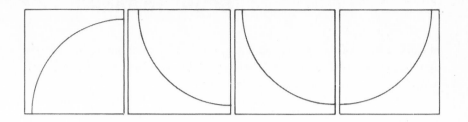

Diction and Style

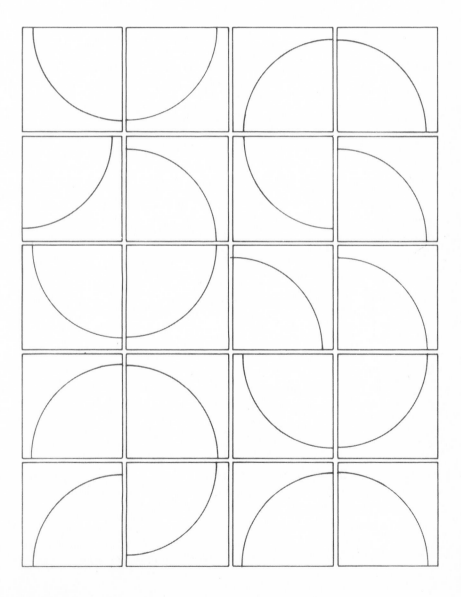

Standard English is the accepted language of English-speaking people. In formal writing, avoid using words that are not considered standard. Always replace nonstandard words in most kinds of prose.

NOT
She was fired up about her new job.

BUT
She was excited about her new job.

Improprieties
Improprieties are the uses of words as the wrong parts of speech or the incorrect uses of words for similar words that have different meanings.

IMPROPRIETY	PROPER FORMS
ice tea (noun for adjective)	iced tea
easy understood (adjective for adverb)	easily understood
except a gift	*accept* a gift
brake a glass	*break* a glass

Idioms
Idioms are accepted expressions with meanings that differ from the meanings of the individual words themselves.

The actor told his co-star to go on stage and *break a leg*. (to do her best)

Many idioms are incorrect because the wrong prepositions are used.

UNIDIOMATIC	IDIOMATIC
conform with	conform to
oblivious of	oblivious to
in reference with	in reference to
the year of 1981	the year 1981

Triteness
Triteness includes worn-out or hackneyed phrases and figures of speech. Substitutes that are fresh and original should be used. Avoid such expressions as the following.

AVOID

if and when	out of the frying pan and into the fire
trials and tribulations	darkness before the dawn
never rains but it pours	putting salt on a wound

   Copyright © 1982 by Houghton Mifflin Company

Correctness

Correct usage requires a knowledge of idioms, the use of a current dictionary, and wide experience with words. Words must be used precisely; writers must avoid using words that are confusing and vague.

The *astrologer* scientifically studied the moons of Jupiter. (The word should be *astronomer.*)

He was in difficult *straights.* (The word should be *straits,* meaning a difficult situation.)

Wordiness

Wordiness is the use of unnecessary words—words that do not improve the reader's understanding of a sentence. Avoid using many words when one or two will serve.

The envelope containing the electric bill was delivered today. (nine words)

The electric bill came today. (five words)

Avoid overuse of the passive voice.

The work done by the carpenter was finished. (eight words)

The carpenter finished the work. (five words)

Revise long sentences to achieve concision.

I wish to say that I have not at this moment fully engaged in this warlike action. (seventeen words)

I have not yet begun to fight. (seven words)

Avoid dependence on *it is, there is,* and *there are.*

It was John Glenn who first orbited the earth in space.

John Glenn first orbited the earth in space.

There are some medicines that have dangerous side effects.

Some medicines have dangerous side effects.

Repetition

Avoid excessive repetition of words, synonyms, and sounds.

The book on the table is a book about buccaneers in the South Seas.

The book on the table is about buccaneers in the South Seas.

The wind sifted sparks from the sizzling blaze.

The wind blew sparks from the blaze.

Copyright © 1982 by Houghton Mifflin Company

Standard English 17.1

▶ *With the aid of a dictionary, label the italicized words (for example,* formal, informal, colloquial, *and so on). Replace substandard expressions with equivalents in standard English.*

EXAMPLE

The businessman *figured* that he could weather the recession by prudent investments.

informal;
concluded

1. Many people consider a legislator who votes his conscience to be a *patsy.*

   _____

2. The Lincoln Memorial is *mighty* impressive any time but especially at night when the crowds have departed.

   _____

3. One can earn *plenty* of extra income by selling scrap aluminum.

   _____

4. Occasionally some misguided *punks* vandalize public property.

   _____

5. The irate coach, *annoyed* by questionable decisions by the officials, decided to protest.

   _____

6. The fear of *bombing out* on an examination may cause a poor performance.

   _____

7. *Bugged* by the heavy traffic along interstate highways, some travelers prefer the more tranquil routes of older, two-lane roads.

   _____

8. The army plans to *beef up* the number of troops now serving the country.

   _____

9. A dictionary is a *right* handy reference book, for it answers questions of usage as well as of meaning.

   _____

10. Hurricanes are *liable* to cause as much water damage as wind damage.

   _____

Copyright © 1982 by Houghton Mifflin Company

Standard English 17.2

▶ *For each of the following supply an appropriate expression in standard English.*

EXAMPLE
nuts ___*psychotic*_____

1. they's _____

2. flunked _____

3. ain't _____

4. messing around _____

5. cop-out _____

6. different than _____

7. gent _____

8. guy _____

9. enthused _____

10. goes to show _____

11. hock _____

12. near enough of _____

13. rap _____

14. would not of _____

15. pan out _____

16. set around _____

17. could of _____

18. irregardless _____

19. being as _____

20. suspicioned _____

Copyright © 1982 by Houghton Mifflin Company

Improprieties   17.3

▶ *Circle improprieties in the following phrases and correct them in the blanks at the right. If you find none, write C in the blank.*

EXAMPLE

(occupation) hazards *occupational* _____

1. reforming institution policies _____

2. averaging students for grades _____

3. dead trees as inhabitants for birds _____

4. Noble Prize _____

5. a dilapidate old house _____

6. a wood mallet _____

7. a wood baseball bat _____

8. a frivolity conversation _____

9. a utopia hideaway _____

10. a utilize room complete with workbench _____

11. the unstabled chemical compounds _____

12. the unskill labor force _____

13. the vandals who rapined Rome _____

14. an erupting volcano crevassing the hills _____

15. criticism writing _____

16. abstracted beyond understanding _____

17. classified as an absorbent _____

18. a handwriting letter _____

19. banjoed their way to the top ten _____

20. a meander stream _____

21. hoboing across the country _____

22. holidayed the time away _____

23. the redirective coming from the officer _____

24. grain-fed slaughter cattle _____

25. ivy tendoned to the walls _____

Copyright © 1982 by Houghton Mifflin Company

Improprieties   17.4

▶ *Choose the correct word and write it in the blank at the right. Consult a dictionary if necessary.*

EXAMPLE

Only (two, to, too) species of the cat family are presently
facing possible extinction in India—the Asian lion and the
Bengal tiger.   *two*_____

1. The (effect, affect) of blight on the nation's chest-
   nut trees was almost complete devastation.   _____

2. A (thorough, through) review of state insurance
   codes should be conducted every five years.   _____

3. The Economic Policy Commission (inferred, im-
   plied) in its announcement that inflation would
   continue.   _____

4. (Continually, Continuously) dripping water
   from a faulty spigot may increase a utility bill.   _____

5. A (principle, principal) cause of the Spanish-
   American War was the sinking of the U.S.S.
   Maine.   _____

6. Lying almost (stationary, stationery) in Havana
   Harbor, the ship suddenly exploded without
   warning.   _____

7. After much (ingenuous, ingenious) research, Admiral Hyman Rickover has recently shown that
   spontaneous combustion was the probable cause
   of the sinking of the *Maine*—not Spanish sabo-
   tage.   _____

8. Dermatologists warn fair- (complected, complex-
   ioned) people not to remain a long time in bright
   sunlight.   _____

9. Sunburn can cause one to (loose, lose) the enjoyment of a vacation at the beach.   _____

10. (Quite, Quiet) often many sun bathers discover that overexposure can be painful.   _____

11. Many begin their vacation under the (allusion, delusion) that they must first burn before they can tan.   _____

12. The sun can burn human skin even on cloudy days; (its, it's) ultraviolet rays easily penetrate cloud cover.   _____

13. The dieter tried to reduce his (wasteline, waistline).   _____

14. The coaching staff of some football teams hire professional psychologists to help motivate (their, there) players.   _____

15. Setting a new record at the marathon was a great (fete, feat) for the runner.   _____

16. (Altering, Altaring) the natural cycle of a forest's development can damage valuable watersheds.   _____

17. (Passed, Past) over by all the political pundits, the darkhorse candidate emerged the winner of the state primary.   _____

18. (Preceding, Proceeding) along migratory routes, wild geese often fly in easily recognizable formations.   _____

19. Physicians (prescribe, proscribe) antibiotics for most respiratory infections.   _____

20. Rapid eye movement indicates continued (psychic, physic) activity after the coming of sleep.   _____

21. Research in (sensual, sensory) perception has made possible the successful teaching of the mentally retarded.   _____

22. The general (moral, morale) of the nation usually increases after a presidential election.   _____

   Copyright © 1982 by Houghton Mifflin Company

23. The delighted parents welcomed their son's (fiancé, fiancée) with warmth and affection. _____

24. The city was (greatful, grateful) for the contributions to the library fund. _____

25. The law rarely accepts the argument that the individual's (conscience, conscious) should be the guide to acceptable social behavior. _____

Copyright © 1982 by Houghton Mifflin Company

Improprieties **17.5**

▶ *Choose the correct word and write it in the blank at the right. Consult a diction-*
ary if necessary.

EXAMPLE
(There, Their) haste was unnecessary.   *Their*

1. The captain of the ship (pored, poured) over the charts. _____

2. The (astrologer, astronomer) helped the astronauts learn to identify the important features of the moon. _____

3. She was very (discrete, discreet) and would never repeat a secret. _____

4. Everyone came to the party (accept, except) me. _____

5. The magician created an interesting (allusion, illusion). _____

6. The chemistry teacher (led, lead) the class to the laboratory. _____

7. The (bare, bear) facts were all they had to help them. _____

8. The prospectors discovered the mother (lode, load) near the top of the canyon. _____

9. The (moral, morale) of the unfortunate travelers was very low. _____

10. The pioneers had (born, borne) many days of trouble before reaching their destination. _____

11. The (plane, plain) the cowboys crossed extends across most of two states. _____

12. I hate to see someone (flout, flaunt) wealth. _____

13. The new producer has recruited writers through-
    out the region and claims they write good (ma-
    terial, materiel).   _____

14. Who is the next of (ken, kin)?   _____

15. His story doesn't (gibe, jibe) with the truth.   _____

16. Many people reject (corporal, corporeal) punish-
    ment.   _____

17. The legislators met at the (capital, capitol).   _____

18. He was immediately struck by an (instinctive,
    intuitive) understanding of the problem and the
    way to solve it.   _____

19. The American language obtains many (lone-
    words, loanwords) from other languages.   _____

20. The passenger paid his (fare, fair) and walked to
    a seat on the bus.   _____

21. The building (site, cite) overlooked the park.   _____

22. When the golfer hit the ball into the woods, he
    cried out, "(Four, Fore)!"   _____

23. The magazine took a (pole, poll) to find out who
    was the most popular movie star.   _____

24. The Academic (Council, Counsel) discussed the
    new curriculum.   _____

25. When the driver's car stalled, she quickly placed
    (flairs, flares) on the highway.   _____

Copyright © 1982 by Houghton Mifflin Company

Idioms 17.6

▶ *Circle faulty idioms in the following sentences. Write correct idioms in the blanks at the right.*

EXAMPLE

Presidential and vice-presidential candidates ideally should feel compatible (to) each other.   *with*

1. In the year of 1922 T. S. Eliot published one of the most influential poems of the century.   _____

2. Contrary with prevailing opinion, most Americans really care very much about the health of their cities.   _____

3. Oblivious of possible dangers, the unpredictable grizzly will charge even a man.   _____

4. Many teachers find that attractive classrooms are conducive of learning.   _____

5. The puma and the wolf were once indigenous of almost every state in the union.   _____

6. The coming election has a bearing with almost all Congressional action.   _____

7. Americans' replies to the challenges of periods of crisis usually are of the affirmative.   _____

8. Often a cash bid for less than the appraised value of some properties will be accepted by brokers.   _____

9. Compared to typical cities of the eighteenth and nineteenth centuries, many modern cities appear relatively clean.   _____

10. Most virologists doubt that we will again experience an epidemic in influenza so widespread as the outbreak during the First World War.   _____

Copyright © 1982 by Houghton Mifflin Company

Idioms 17.7

▶ *Circle faulty idioms in the following sentences. Write correct idioms in the blanks at the right. Write C if the idiom is correct.*

EXAMPLE

This book compares computers (with) the human brain.   *to*

1. He would of done that.   _____

2. Our quiet, shady street is similar with the one in the new motion picture.   _____

3. The civic club wanted to try and do something nice for senior citizens.   _____

4. The driver was ignorant to the traffic regulation in England.   _____

5. The boxers inside of the ring waited for the sound of the bell.   _____

6. People had not ought to try to cheat on their taxes.   _____

7. The trip was not all that interesting.   _____

8. The reason the dam broke is because of the heavy spring rains.   _____

9. In regards to the city's problems, the mayor will call a council meeting.   _____

10. Political candidates often win elections by using their ability to charm and flatter the voters.   _____

248

Copyright © 1982 by Houghton Mifflin Company

Triteness   17.8

▶ *Revise the following sentences to eliminate triteness.*

EXAMPLE

Off the field, the huge defensive end is like a bull in a china shop.

Off the field, the huge defensive end is awkward and destructive.

1. Many historians find that their best primary sources are, first and foremost, old family letters saved from time immemorial.

   _____

   _____

   _____

   _____

2. City planners must never forget that Rome was not built in a day and that public acceptance of their ideas requires time.

   _____

   _____

   _____

   _____

3. When their ideas fall on deaf ears, these planners must continue to put their shoulders to the wheel, so to speak, and refuse to give up.

   _____

   _____

   _____

   _____

4. "You have bought during a declining market," said the doleful

stockbroker to his disheartened client, "but if at first you don't succeed, try, try again."

_____

_____

_____

5. San Francisco, a city that was rebuilt after suffering the effects of a devastating earthquake, is proof that every cloud has a silver lining.

_____

_____

_____

6. Old diaries, journals, and letters reveal that the early pioneers in the West found some of the wild country to be pretty as a picture.

_____

_____

_____

7. The chief targets of confidence men are gullible investors who continue to believe that there is a pot of gold at the end of the rainbow.

_____

_____

_____

8. While traveling down the highway of life, one must remember that virtue is its own reward.

_____

_____

_____

   Copyright © 1982 by Houghton Mifflin Company

9. The thrust of most economists' complaints is that short-range political considerations take precedence over long-range economic policy.

_____

_____

_____

_____

10. The premises of international diplomacy are that the pen is mightier than the sword and that a soft answer turneth away wrath.

_____

_____

_____

_____

Copyright © 1982 by Houghton Mifflin Company

Triteness   17.9

▶ *Revise the following sentences to eliminate triteness.*

EXAMPLE

Everyone on the team was happy as a lark.

Everyone on the team was pleased with the victory.

1. Famous authors are often considered to be sharp as a tack.

   _____

   _____

2. The United States traditionally has been in the forefront of medical research.

   _____

   _____

   _____

3. Superstars of the college sports scene, in a manner of speaking, can write their own tickets in professional sports.

   _____

   _____

   _____

4. The first British colonists in America quickly learned that charity and neighborliness were necessary to keep the ball rolling.

   _____

   _____

   _____

5. A few of these first colonists gave up the ship and returned to England, but most never lost heart.

   _____

   _____

   _____

6. Those willing to travel in the wee hours of the morning usually spend less for airline fares.

_____

_____

_____

7. Older children are often green with envy when their younger siblings receive most of a parent's attention.

_____

_____

_____

8. The main duty of the public health officer is to nip communicable diseases in the bud.

_____

_____

_____

9. Truly great leaders are few and far between, and even when they appear on the scene, they may not rock the boat.

_____

_____

_____

10. Victims of natural catastrophes must convince themselves that it is always darkest before the dawn and that, if winter comes, spring cannot be far behind.

_____

_____

_____

Copyright © 1982 by Houghton Mifflin Company

Wordiness 17.10

▶ *Revise the following sentences to make them concise.*

EXAMPLE

~~In her time~~ Marie Curie was one of the most important persons of her age.

1. It was William Harvey who first wrote about the circulation of the blood.

   _____

   _____

2. Few series have been as popular with the reading public as the books on Captain Horatio Hornblower.

   _____

   _____

3. To be sure, Benjamin Franklin was not, as it were, a great writer, but he was, to all intents and purposes, a great man, more or less.

   _____

   _____

   _____

4. Americans have always applauded the tenacious underdog who is down but who tries to recover and help himself.

   _____

   _____

   _____

5. All human beings possess certain doctrines of natural rights which have been instituted by nature.

   _____

   _____

   _____

6. As anybody can see, most Americans have been affected by television in such a way that their appreciation of the arts has obviously become less and less.

_____

_____

_____

7. In comparing college with high school, from both the educational and the social standpoints, one will find there are indeed many differences.

_____

_____

_____

8. In the times in which we live, a man just can hardly be independent any longer. Look what is happening to him in the field of education. People virtually dictate to him about his economic theories. This is also true even in his personal philosophy of life.

_____

_____

_____

_____

9. A basic and fundamental idea that each student should have in mind is the idea of what good and bad study habits are. The lack of this knowledge is one of the main factors in causing students to fail in school.

_____

_____

_____

_____

10. The most fundamental and primary thing that anyone can possibly say about the pragmatic method is that it is a method of settling

Copyright © 1982 by Houghton Mifflin Company

very abstract, abstruse, and subtle disputes that otherwise might last, or at least seem as if they would last, forever.

Copyright © 1982 by Houghton Mifflin Company

Wordiness 17.11

▶ *Revise the following sentences to make them concise.*

EXAMPLE

I came for the reason that I was hungry.

I came because I was hungry.

1. The functional sections of a modern camera are directly analogous to the basic biological divisions in the human eye.

   _____

   _____

   _____

2. A periodonist is a dentist who has decided to specialize in diseases of the gums.

   _____

   _____

   _____

3. The author's writings contain many short, brief sentences that express broad, basic truths and are very readable.

   _____

   _____

   _____

4. No one can deny that hunting big game with a camera is fully as dangerous as hunting big game with a rifle.

   _____

   _____

   _____

5. An ovenbird is an American bird which is a member of the warbler

family and which builds a nest that resembles an oven on the floor of a forest.

_____

_____

_____

6. In many ways certain cities retained and still do retain a small-town atmosphere in those neighborhoods characterized by unique ethnic charm and lifestyles.

_____

_____

_____

7. For years and years the basic cultural foundations of this great nation was the small town with its small, homogeneous neighborhoods and communal cohesion.

_____

_____

_____

8. Beginning in the 1930s and continuing through several decades down to the present time, writers have often been interested in Hollywood as a setting for their novels.

_____

_____

_____

_____

9. Oil painting in modern America is an art medium of creative expression which is presently enjoyed by many amateurs and other people who paint although they often do not know a great deal about oil painting.

_____

_____

_____

_____

Copyright © 1982 by Houghton Mifflin Company

10. Two breeds of dogs that are generally considered by most authorities as good guard dogs are the Doberman pinscher and the German shepherd, and these two breeds may, without difficulty, be compared and contrasted on the grounds of appearance, disposition, and physical prowess.

Copyright © 1982 by Houghton Mifflin Company

Wordiness 17.12

▶ *Revise the following sentences to make them concise.*

1. It is a known and proven fact that run-off elections draw fewer voters than regular elections.

   _____

   _____

   _____

2. The definition of tragedy, as one might expect, evolves and changes along with the basic moral values of various societies.

   _____

   _____

   _____

3. A single measure using a spoon filled with sugar expedites the ingestion of pharmaceuticals.

   _____

   _____

   _____

4. Current research on the nervous system of the cockroach, of all things, might just conceivably lead to a cure for glaucoma, a disease of the eye.

   _____

   _____

   _____

   _____

5. Major political pollsters are presently worried about the definite trend of so many people to refuse to answer questionaires or to take part in interviews.

   _____

_____

_____

_____

6. Some birdfeeders differ in various ways from others because various birds have different eating habits and feeding requirements, and it is just that simple.

_____

_____

_____

_____

7. Mammoths were prehistoric beasts that looked like elephants with very hairy skin and that often measured eleven feet at the shoulders with tusks as long as thirteen feet.

_____

_____

_____

_____

8. Laws requiring motorcycle riders to wear crash helmets have saved, beyond any doubt or question, many lives in the past and will most certainly account for the saving of many lives in the future.

_____

_____

_____

_____

9. Our present-day, or Gregorian, calendar is based on the Julian calendar, which was established by that famous Roman emperor Julius Caesar and which fixed the length of the year at 365 days.

_____

_____

_____

_____

10. Many people feel that it is probably best to employ those electricians and plumbers who are licensed because they then know that

Copyright © 1982 by Houghton Mifflin Company

the work performed almost always will be bonded by an insurance company.

_____

_____

_____

_____

Copyright © 1982 by Houghton Mifflin Company

Repetition 17.13

▷ *Revise the following sentences to eliminate ineffective repetition.*

EXAMPLE

Driving winds *drove* the sailors toward the beach.

High winds drove the sailors toward the beach.

1. Instant replays show that officials usually make correct calls and perform their duties both correctly and responsibly.

2. After the bear market of the early 1970s, stockbrokers decided to diversify and to market various other securities other than common stocks.

3. The danger of dense cloud cover in densely traveled air corridors is a midair collision.

4. Most large cities are circumscribed by large beltways that prevent large traffic jams.

5. The situation comedy that is interesting, engaging, and prepossessing will always attract and engage a television audience.

_____

_____

_____

6. The respected judge of a debate never allows contempt or scorn or disparagement or derision to be displayed on the debate floor.

_____

_____

_____

7. Sewing one's own clothes is a way of saving money and allows one to choose one's favorite style and one's favorite fabric.

_____

_____

_____

8. Successful football teams that win often have kickers who kick field goals and kick extra points well.

_____

_____

_____

9. The alert insurance adjustor must be constantly alert to improper evidence of impropriety or fraud, while never forgetting to be fair, equitable, and just.

_____

_____

_____

_____

10. Farmers' markets are enjoying a good resurgence in larger cities;

 Copyright © 1982 by Houghton Mifflin Company

on good days, a farmer in New York or Seattle or Santa Fe or Boston may gross a thousand dollars.

_____

_____

_____

_____

Copyright © 1982 by Houghton Mifflin Company

Repetition   17.14

▶ *Revise the following sentences to eliminate ineffective repetition.*

EXAMPLE

Producers who *produce* useful *products* stay in business.

Manufacturers of useful products stay in business.

1. Erupting volcanoes erupt with terrific force, spewing hot, molten lava and scattering volcanic ash for miles and miles and miles.

   _____

   _____

   _____

2. Floods that flood fields and flood croplands are ever-present dangers to the farmer.

   _____

   _____

   _____

3. Powdery snow on ski slopes must be monitored constantly for loose powdery density and possible snowslides.

   _____

   _____

   _____

4. Small bark beetles bear a fungus that causes a disease which attacks the Dutch elm tree.

   _____

   _____

   _____

5. Fashion designers sometimes fashion their designs after the traditional dress of nomadic tribes.

_____

_____

_____

6. Horizontal stripes on clothes emphasize heaviness and are shunned by heavy people.

_____

_____

_____

7. The climbing high prices of new cars will climb higher and higher before they level off.

_____

_____

_____

8. Sand painting, the ancient art of painting pictures with colored sand, was first originated by American Indians for their ancient rituals.

_____

_____

_____

9. Some elk from overpopulated elk herds in Yellowstone National Park have been exported to other parks in other regions and even to other countries.

_____

_____

_____

_____

10. Charcoal, first used as a filter in gasmasks during the First World

   Copyright © 1982 by Houghton Mifflin Company

War, filters the air in submarines and spacecraft and also filters automobile emissions.

Connotation, Figurative Language, and Vocabulary   18

Connotation

Words often have special associations and meanings called **connotations.** In addition, **denotations** of words are their precise meanings. Denotatively, the word *home* simply refers to a dwelling place. Connotatively, the word suggests several emotional reactions relating to family, friends, and special occasions.

Good writers attempt to find words that have the right associations—those that work most effectively.

EXAMPLE

Fred is a *funny* person. (*funny* is weak because it is too general.)

IMPROVED

Fred is *witty*.

Fred is a *practical joker*.

Fred is a *great impersonator*.

Figurative language

Avoid mixed and inappropriate figures of speech. Mixed figures associate things that are not logically related.

EXAMPLE

He stumbled along like a car in heavy traffic. (Cars cannot *stumble*.)

Use figurative comparisons to create originality.

EXAMPLE

Language is the cornerstone of civilization. (metaphor)

Opportunity is *like* a good mystery story; you never know what will happen when you turn the page. (simile)

Flowery language

Avoid ornate or pretentious language. Make your sentences clear.

PLAIN LANGUAGE	FLOWERY LANGUAGE
today	in this world in which we live and work
pen	this writing instrument
finally	having reached the termination of this discourse

Copyright © 1982 by Houghton Mifflin Company

NAME _____

DATE _____ SCORE _____

▶ *Words which have approximately the same denotation frequently suggest mean-*
ings that are different. The combinations that follow bring together words with
different connotations. In the spaces at right, rate each word in terms of its favor-
ability of connotation—1 for most favorable, 2 for less favorable, and 3 for least
favorable. Be prepared to defend your decisions and to explain the different
shades of connotation.

EXAMPLE

abdomen _____1_____

stomach _____2_____

belly _____3_____

1. ill _____
   sick _____
   diseased _____

2. overweight _____
   fat _____
   stout _____

3. economical _____
   stingy _____
   thrifty _____

4. abnormal _____
   eccentric _____
   peculiar _____

5. extremist _____
   fanatic _____
   enthusiast _____

6. garbage _____
   rubbish _____
   trash _____

7. quixotic _____
   romantic _____
   impractical _____

8. murder _____
   kill _____
   execute _____

9. decay _____
   rot _____
   decompose _____

10. stern _____
    severe _____
    harsh _____

INSTRUCTIONAL SERVICE CENTER

11. wither   _____   virtuoso   _____

     languish   _____   19. vulture   _____

     shrivel   _____   scavenger   _____

12. simple   _____   buzzard   _____

     naive   _____   20. boat   _____

     innocent   _____   ship   _____

13. impulsive   _____   liner   _____

     spontaneous   _____   21. lie   _____

     unconstrained   _____   deception   _____

14. famous   _____   falsehood   _____

     notorious   _____   22. visionary   _____

     well-known   _____   dreamer   _____

15. aged   _____   romancer   _____

     mellow   _____   23. illegal   _____

     nature   _____   unlawful   _____

16. food   _____   criminal   _____

     meat   _____   24. ignoble   _____

     victuals   _____   vile   _____

17. automobile   _____   disreputable   _____

     car   _____   25. request   _____

     limousine   _____   solicit   _____

18. singer   _____   beg   _____

     vocalist   _____

Copyright © 1982 by Houghton Mifflin Company

Connotation 18.2

▶ *Words which have approximately the same denotation frequently suggest mean-*
ings that are different. The combinations that follow bring together words with
different connotations. In the spaces at right, rate each word in terms of its favor-
ability of connotation—1 for most favorable, 2 for less favorable, and 3 for least
favorable. Be prepared to defend your decisions and to explain the different
shades of connotation.

1. perseverance _____   hurt _____

   obstinacy _____   8. evict _____

   doggedness_____   remove _____

2. merchandise _____   oust _____

   hawk _____   9. watch_____

   peddle _____   ogle _____

3. resist _____   stare _____

   defy _____   10. antipathy _____

   oppose _____   disgust _____

4. distinguished_____   aversion_____

   noted _____   11. repine _____

   renowned _____   grieve_____

5. angry_____   fret_____

   mad _____   12. anesthetic _____

   wrathful_____   dope _____

6. abode _____   drug _____

   home _____   13. artless _____

   habitation _____   unsophisticated _____

7. offended_____   ordinary_____

   insulted _____   14. ignorant_____

dumb _____

uninformed _____

15. clothed _____

    attired _____

    dressed _____

16. awkward _____

    bungling _____

    incompetent _____

17. dress _____

    frock _____

    gown _____

18. puny _____

    little _____

    small _____

19. plea _____

    argue _____

    exhort _____

20. despondency _____

dejection _____

gloom _____

21. probity _____

    candor _____

    frankness _____

22. horde _____

    crowd _____

    mob _____

23. alarming _____

    frightful _____

    scary _____

24. fat _____

    obese _____

    corpulent _____

25. imitation _____

    counterfeit _____

    sham _____

Copyright © 1982 by Houghton Mifflin Company

Figurative Language 18.3

▶ *Here is a descriptive passage from Francis Parkman's* The Oregon Trail. *Fill in the blanks using the following list of Parkman's figures of speech and images.*

bellowed and growled	beat down	
whirling sheets	black heads	leaped out quivering
cataracts	deep muttering	long rolling peal
accompaniment	to roll hoarsely	piles of cotton

It was late that morning before we were on the march; and early in the afternoon we were compelled to encamp, for a thunder-gust came up and suddenly enveloped us in [1] _____ of rain. With much ado we pitched our tents amid the tempest, and all night long the thunder [2] _____ over our heads. In the morning light peaceful showers succeeded the [3] _____ of rain, that had been drenching us through the canvas of our tents. About noon, when there were some treacherous indications of fair weather, we got in motion again.

Not a breath of air stirred over the free and open prairie; the clouds were like light [4] _____; and where the blue sky was visible, it wore a hazy and languid aspect. The sun [5] _____ upon us with a sultry, penetrating heat almost insupportable, and as our party crept slowly along over the interminable level, the horses hung their heads as they waded fetlock deep through the mud, and the men slouched into the easiest position upon the saddle. At last, towards evening, the old familiar [6] _____ of thunder-clouds rose fast above the horizon, and the same [7] _____ of distant thunder that had become the ordinary [8] _____ of our afternoon's journey began [9] _____ over the prairie. Only a few minutes elapsed before the whole sky was densely shrouded, and the prairie and some clusters of woods in front assumed a purple hue beneath the inky shadows. Suddenly from the densest fold of the cloud the flash [10] _____ again and again down to the edge of the prairie; and at the same instant came the sharp burst and the [11] _____ of the thunder. A cool wind, filled with the smell of rain, just then overtook us, levelling the tall grass by the side of the path.

Copyright © 1982 by Houghton Mifflin Company

Flowery Language 18.4

▶ *Revise the following sentences to eliminate flowery language.*

EXAMPLE

The inside of a geode glitters with the silvery radiance of sidereal splendor.

The inside of a geode sparkles with crystals.

1. One contumelious guest may ruin an affair of convivial celebration.

_____

_____

2. Seraphic warblers intone the roseate commencement of glorious spring.

_____

_____

3. Many cardiologists advise a swift retreat from the ambrosial condiments of the evening repast.

_____

_____

4. Elegant garbs of sartorial splendor often disguise patrician parsimony.

_____

_____

5. Many poets have been inspired by the vision of artless, cherubic children gamboling like sylvan nymphs over the verdurous sward.

_____

_____

_____

6. With the coming of golden autumn the cultivators of the earth garner the blessings of Ceres.

_____

_____

_____

7. The venerable institution of holy matrimony has become the object of much sociological research in the hallowed halls of academia.

_____

_____

_____

8. Rafters down the mighty Mississippi watercourse provide the sonorous, nocturnal chorus of bullfrogs with a spirited audience.

_____

_____

_____

9. The pied clouds of pastel hues served notice that the strong winds had given way to the wings of gentle zephyrs.

_____

_____

_____

10. A major expenditure of institutions of higher learning is for the construction and maintenance of campus edifices to domicile young questers for truth and beauty.

_____

_____

_____

Copyright © 1982 by Houghton Mifflin Company

Vocabulary 18.5

▶ *In the blank at the right, place the letter of the word or phrase you believe is nearest in meaning to the italicized word.*

EXAMPLE

He has a *paramour:* (a) small tractor, (b) virtue, (c) illicit lover _____c_____

1. a *defunct* issue: (a) overdrawn, (b) boring, (c) dead _____

2. an *assiduous* student: (a) diligent, (b) well-read, (c) skeptical _____

3. an *innocuous* potion: (a) poisonous, (b) harmless, (c) powerful _____

4. a *quixotic* character: (a) questioning, (b) variable, (c) visionary _____

5. a *lethargic* river: (a) sluggish, (b) polluted, (c) deep _____

6. a *niggardly* church member: (a) prejudiced, (b) stingy, (c) swarthy _____

7. the *nadir* of my life: (a) abomination, (b) highest point, (c) lowest point _____

8. a *gratuitous* insult: (a) unwarranted, (b) deserved, (c) vehement _____

9. their *heterodox* beliefs: (a) spiritual, (b) conservative, (c) heretical _____

10. a *verbose* lecturer: (a) dynamic, (b) wordy, (c) boring _____

11. please *elucidate:* (a) explain, (b) denounce, (c) arrange _____

12. an *omnivorous* being: (a) immortal, (b) eating all kinds of food, (c) knowing everything _____

13. Behold the *firmament:* (a) earth, (b) sky, (c) fortification _____

14. to *opt* for freedom: (a) decide, (b) flee, (c) sing   ———

15. a *disparate* group of people: (a) essentially different, (b) dangerous, (c) capable of murder   ———

16. a *proletarian:* (a) wage-earner, (b) revolutionary, (c) democrat   ———

17. a *laconic* reply: (a) heated, (b) ill-advised, (c) concise   ———

18. an *exigent* situation: (a) demanding, (b) deceased, (c) absent   ———

19. the beloved *prelate:* (a) actor, (b) grandparent, (c) church dignitary   ———

20. a *choleric* temperament: (a) sickly, (b) irascible, (c) morose   ———

Copyright © 1982 by Houghton Mifflin Company

Vocabulary 18.6

▶ *In the blank at the right, place the letter of the word or phrase you believe is nearest in meaning to the italicized word.*

EXAMPLE

He gave a *laconic* reply: (a) heated; (b) ill-advised; (c) concise _c_

1. an *aquiline* nose: (a) hooked, (b) long, (c) snub _____

2. *desultory* talk: (a) insulting, (b) boring, (c) random _____

3. a *malignant* plan: (a) ineffective, (b) evil, (c) terminal _____

4. an *overt* act: (a) subversive, (b) hostile, (c) open to view _____

5. a hunched *Mephistopheles:* (a) ogre, (b) devil, (c) Greek god _____

6. a *crucial* year: (a) disturbing, (b) painful, (c) decisive _____

7. a needed *admonition:* (a) reproof, (b) falsehood, (c) compliment _____

8. a *facetious* remark: (a) obvious, (b) witty, (c) angry _____

9. a *voluptuous* woman: (a) sensual, (b) plump, (c) adulterous _____

10. the *acrimonious* controversy: (a) bitter, (b) marital, (c) religious _____

11. an *ineradicable* mark: (a) disfiguring, (b) black, (c) indelible _____

12. feeling *nauseous:* (a) sickening, (b) sick, (c) ridiculous _____

13. a *strident* voice: (a) low, (b) shrill, (c) stuttering _____

14. devices of *propaganda:* (a) spreading ideas, (b) lies, (c) politics _____

15. the *inherent* supremacy of human beings: (a) natural, (b) unnatural; (c) immoral _____

16. an *anachronism:* (a) severe deformity, (b) event placed in the wrong time, (c) an enigma _____

17. a human *fetus:* (a) unborn child, (b) abortion, (c) corpse ———

18. a *swarthy* villain: (a) sneaky, (b) greasy, (c) dark-complexioned ———

19. to *refute* an argument: (a) summarize, (b) disprove, (c) begin ———

20. to treat with *levity:* (a) gaiety, (b) seriousness, (c) haste ———

Copyright © 1982 by Houghton Mifflin Company

Paragraph Unity: Topic Sentences 19.1

▶ *Divide the following passage into paragraphs by inserting the sign ¶. The original passage contains three paragraphs. Underline topic sentences, and in the blanks at the end of the passage, write briefly in your own words the controlling idea of the paragraph.*

If country music, like soul and Latin music, remains a securely delineated subgenre within pop, there are signs of erosion of that purity. The hope, as well as the fear, in Nashville these days is the "crossover," or the leap of a country song onto the national pop sales charts, and hence from relatively modest success to the millions to be made when the big pop AM stations all over the country start playing and propagating a record. The hope is that a country singer can reach that wider acclaim. The fear is that, in so doing, the artist may dilute his style past recognizability. And, further, there is fear that the process can work the other way—the supposed country charts in recent years have often been topped by such artists as John Denver, Olivia Newton-John, and Linda Ronstadt. They may be singing outwardly country songs, but they are hardly country in either their biographies or their links to Nashville musical institutions. The whole crossover phenomenon provides an obvious musical metaphor for Southern culture and its relation to the rest of America: crossover success means recognition on a national level even as the indigenous roots that nourish that success are eroded. Needless to say, many older forms of country music remain vital parts of our folk culture today. What distinguishes them from mainstream country and what helps assure their traditional purity is their very freedom from commercialism. There are some established country stars who consciously revert to the Anglo-American folk tradition that underlies all country music. But the many folk festivals around the country are full of eager "string bands"—fiddle-dominated ensembles that trace their ancestry back through the crudely amplified fiddle groups of the Depression to the traditional country and mountain ensembles of the nineteenth century. This music goes by a variety of overlapping names— "mountain music," "old-timey music"—that often refer to similar music with only minor regional variants. The best-known form of such older music is bluegrass, popularized by Eric Weissberg with his music for the film *Deliverance*. Bluegrass is actually of fairly recent invention, for all its debts to older forms of folkcountry, and its inventors, Bill Monroe and the Bluegrass Boys, are still regaling audiences with their blend of quick-stepping tempos, exuberant fiddle playing, and high, hard tenorizing. More recently, Earl Scruggs, once the banjo-playing half of the Flatt and Scruggs duo, has attempted to broaden bluegrass's appeal by allying it with quasi-rock instrumentation.

—John Rockwell,
"Blues, and Other Noises, in the Night"

CONTROLLING IDEAS

1. _____

_____

2. _____

_____

3. _____

_____

Copyright © 1982 by Houghton Mifflin Company

Paragraph Unity: Topic Sentences   19.2

▶ *Divide the following passage into paragraphs by inserting the sign ¶. The original passage contains three paragraphs. Underline topic sentences, and in the blanks at the end of the passage, write briefly in your own words the controlling idea of the paragraph.*

After a musical has opened in New York and has had the rare privilege of getting unanimous raves from the critics, everyone from the producers, writers, and directors right on down to the chorus relaxes to bask in the sunlight of critical acceptance, public support, and financial gain. The dancers, especially, enjoy the hit in a strange sort of way. They immediately go back to the strenuous activity of daily jazz and ballet classes, masochistically stretching and twisting in order to stay in shape for auditions when this show eventually closes. After the strenuous activity of daytime classes, the theatre often becomes a place to rest up and recuperate for tomorrow's classes. Out come the magazines, books, knitting, and small change for poker games, and even possibly TV with the sound turned way down; the whole thing takes on the atmosphere of a USO. At this point the management, in the flush of success, decides that it can afford an extra dancer to cover the possibility that dancers will be out sick from time to time.

—Bob Evans,
"How to Get a Job as a 'Swing Dancer' in a Hit Broadway Show"

CONTROLLING IDEAS

1. _____

   _____

2. _____

   _____

3. _____

   _____

Copyright © 1982 by Houghton Mifflin Company

Paragraph Unity: Digressive Sentences   19.3

▶ *Write unified paragraphs. Be sure that every sentence is related to the topic. In the blanks at the left, write the number of any sentence that is digressive. In any paragraph there may be as many as three such sentences.*

EXAMPLE

(1) To use a library efficiently one must first learn how books are classified in the card catalog. (2) Card catalogs are located usually on a library's main floor—but not always. (3) Books are listed in three ways: by author, by title, and by subject. (4) Thus if one knows a title, but not an author or a subject, one can easily locate a book.

A.   (1) One of the most overused words used today is "major." (2) This is not the army or marine rank. (3) No company would dare list a new program as a "minor" one. (4) And what politician would ever deliver a "short talk"? (5) No, any speech no matter how insignificant must be labeled a "major address to the American people." (6) Thus "major" takes its place alongside "startling new discovery" and the many other expressions that have undermined our language.

_____

B.   (1) Financial aid for students includes basic grants, work-study jobs, scholarships, and loans. (2) In the past, students who required financial assistance often had to drop out of school and work for a few months. (3) Many students simultaneously receive aid from several of these sources, usually combining scholarships with work-study programs. (4) College administrations continually solicit alumni for more money. (5) Jobs are especially popular because they may provide valuable experience for a future vocation. (6) Some of the country's most distinguished citizens received scholarships. (7) All students in need of financial assistance qualify for aid in one form or another. (8) Even if they must borrow from university loan funds, they usually pay only minimal interest charges. (9) Students who desire assistance should contact their school's financial aid office for further information.

_____

C.   (1) Almost any backyard can be transformed into a showcase wildlife habitat. (2) Birdfeeders, birdbaths, small fishponds—all combined with the right shrubs and trees will attract a variety of wildlife. (3) Many neighbors may want to transform their yards as well. (4) Now several species of wildlife are steadily losing their natural habitat to industry and agriculture. (5) Shrubs (such as hawthorne, crab apple, and silky dogwood) and hardwood trees (like oak or beech) serve small animals and many songbirds. (6) In addition, colorful annual flowers attract many helpful insects. (7) If enough fresh water is available, ducks, raccoons, frogs, and crayfish will soon visit. (8) Backyard ecology is especially popular among the youth.

_____

D.   (1) To see the Grand Canyon as it should be seen, a visitor must rise before dawn. (2) The canyon is located in northern Arizona. (3) Just before the sun appears the walls of the canyon are a deep purple, and a visitor almost feels the eerie silence. (4) Gradually the canyon comes alive. (5) Soon there are the cries of a few birds. (6) Then with the first streaks of light, the rocks begin to glow in rich oranges and reds. (7) Finally, the details appear—the deep crevices, the patches of grass and mesquite and sage—and a visitor who looks closely may see a deer or chipmunk. (8) Later the visitor can visit the many shops located near Bright Angel Lodge and El Tovar.

_____

E.   (1) The great cities before Rome—Corinth, Carthage, Syracuse—were trading and manufacturing centers. (2) Rome, on the other hand, was the financial and political capital of the Western world. (3) Rome never rivaled previous great cities in commerce or industry. (4) Another great city of the ancient world was Carthage, located in North Africa. (5) Rome usually imported most of its necessities and luxuries from cities and regions under its military and political control. (6) Sicily and Africa especially provided for Rome's agricultural needs such as corn. (7) During the so-called Golden Age of Greece, Athens was the intellectual center of Western civilization.

_____

F.   (1) What does the television mean to the American family? (2) Many people enjoy westerns, comedies, and detective shows. (3) Ask those who work at home what they enjoy on television and learn the sordid details in the lives of every character on "As the World Turns" and "All My Children." (4) Ask any husband which comes first—the news or dinner—and hear how important it is to keep informed by watching Roger Mudd report from Washington. (5) And how many of us have heard some child wail, "I don't have anything to do!" when

    Copyright © 1982 by Houghton Mifflin Company

the TV is at the shop? (6) One can only wonder if our founding fathers ever could have envisioned television as our principal means to achieve "life, liberty, and the pursuit of happiness."

G.   (1) The modern photographer needs more than a simple developing kit to process photographs at home. (2) Actually, processing photographs at home is probably more expensive than having professional laboratories develop them. (3) The most important and most expensive item required for film processing is a good enlarger. (4) If one develops negatives without an enlarger, then the final pictures are almost too small to enjoy. (5) Used enlargers for sale are very difficult to find. (6) Furthermore, one should purchase an enlarging easel, an enlarger timer, and a focusing lens. (7) Only after buying this relatively expensive equipment can the amateur photographer hope to develop good-quality prints.

H.   (1) Many expressions have been used to describe the second half of the twentieth century. (2) With enormous arrogance we have called our brief period in history the nuclear age or the age of progress and cavalierly ignored any improvements in the human lot that were produced over the last several thousand years. (3) Perhaps we should reassess our view of ourselves and look a bit to the world we inherited. (4) Moreover, we have created more waste, expended more of the earth's natural resources, spent more money and time on frivolities and entertainment, and—as far as we can see into the future at this moment—left generations to come with greater problems to solve than any previous generation left to its successors in the entire span of human history. (5) We have proclaimed this the era of progress, but future generations may one day mock us for our vanity. (6) We should all try to improve our environment.

I.   (1) Archeology is a much more exact science than many people realize. (2) For example, archeologists have determined that, on a day in late spring approximately 400,000 years ago, about twenty-five people made a brief visit to a cove on the Mediterranean coast near Nice, France. (3) From the study of fossil bones, stone tools, various imprints in the sand, and the density of the sand, scientists have reconstructed in detail much of the three-day sojourn. (4) Imprints give clues to where these ancient people slept and what they slept on. (5) Archeology has really matured as a science and has become quite popular in the public's eye since Heinrich Schliemann's excavation of ancient cities in the latter nineteenth century. (6) These imaginative scientists also know much about the food these nomadic people ate, how they prepared it, how they hunted for food, and how they protected the group from predators at night. (7) The human imagination simply has no limits.

———————————

J. (1) When people complain about the outlandish fashions of the great contemporary American and French designers, someone should remind them that this is not the only age to flaunt the outrageous in wearing apparel. (2) These clothes may be purchased at most major department stores and in many boutiques across the country. (3) For sheer absurdity we only have to look to the zoot suit of the 1940s, or, if we are truly interested in the bizarre, we might remember the bustle and bloomers. (4) No age has been without its oddities. (5) We can only be thankful that so few of them became permanent additions to our wardrobes.

———————————

    Copyright © 1982 by Houghton Mifflin Company

Paragraph Unity: Transitions　19.4

▶ *Underline once the main transitional devices (transitional words, repeated words, pronouns, and demonstrative adjectives) that enable the reader to see connections between clauses and sentences. Underline twice those that enable the reader to see the connections between paragraphs.*

When students complete a first draft, they consider the job of writing done—and their teachers too often agree. When professional writers complete a first draft, they usually feel that they are at the start of the writing process. When a draft is completed, the job of writing can begin.

That difference in attitude is the difference between amateur and professional, inexperience and experience, journeyman and craftsman. Peter F. Drucker, the prolific business writer, calls his first draft "the zero draft"—after that he can start counting. Most writers share the feeling that the first draft, and all of those which follow, are opportunities to discover what they have to say and how best they can say it.

To produce a progression of drafts, each of which says more and says it more clearly, the writer has to develop a special kind of reading skill. In school we are taught to decode what appears on the page as finished writing. Writers, however, face a different category of possibility and responsibility when they read their own drafts. To them the words on the page are never finished. Each can be changed and rearranged, can set off a chain reaction of confusion or clarified meaning. This is a different kind of reading which is possibly more difficult and certainly more exciting.

—Donald M. Murray,
"The Maker's Eye: Revising Your Own Manuscripts"

Cross-References to the *Practical English Handbook,* Sixth Edition